Sons

of

Suicide

a memoir of friendship

steely poet
My earliest experience
was being left... but
Maybe I've not paid
enough attn to
the one

Richard J. Knapp & J. David Pincus

who has stayed...
tho she'll leave me, too

ISBN 978-1-7338287-0-3

If you or anyone you know is
struggling with thoughts
of suicide and needs help,
here is the number to call, 24/7...

Readers React to Sons of Suicide...

What clinicians and counselors have said...

"Soon after reading your manuscript, I started to see a new client, a single mother of a 13-year-old boy. She has been contemplating suicide for quite some time. Your words are with me as I speak with her . . ."

"Your stories give other sons of suicide validation, and encourage deeper reflection, an important element of healing."

— *Nicole Kent, Ph.D.*, clinical psychologist

"...a beautiful story, engaging, open and honest. It does an excellent job highlighting paths to the healing process. Your stories give other sons of suicide validation and encourage deeper reflection, an important element of healing . . . I work with children and adults and believe that open, honest talk is important for all ages."

— *Dr. Lance Foster, M.D.*, child, adolescent and adult psychiatrist

"You get to the heart of the issues suicide brings up in families and adult children. It is a very human story, told in an interesting and perceptive manner that will resonate with people who have suffered trauma – will help them see they are not alone and that others have experienced the same feelings. I admire your courage in writing this and how hard it was getting yourselves healthy after suffering such devastating losses. Thank you for allowing me to enter your world through the book . . ."

— *Terry Luria*, clinical director, Stella Maris, Cleveland

What survivors of tragic loss have said . . .

". . . an important and impactful book for so many to read!"

— *Ann Meyers Drysdale*, *pro basketball Hall of Fame player, Olympic medalist, and business executive whose life has been touched by suicide*

"I can't think of many men who have had the kind of profound and long-term relationship that you two have shared . . . few men have this kind of easy grace around emotional subjects. I am really grateful for the insights *Sons of Suicide* gave me."

"After my husband's death, it was so clear to me that I had one job – to help my daughter begin to make sense around something that is senseless. I didn't have a clue how to do that, but we were walking the path together. Children of suicide must feel so untethered, especially if there is no other parent to demonstrate that there are still ties that hold them in place . . . I think a key point of this book is that you provided those ties to each other."

— *Anne O'Leary-Kelly, Ph.D.*, *survivor of suicide loss*

". . .very well written with lots of details and life experiences. For me, it's been 11 years and it still opened up raw emotions – but in a positive way, and made me reflect and realize that my feelings are not unique. The book also reaffirms the importance of grief groups and finding people to bond with."

— *Rosemarie Owens*, *survivor of suicide loss*

"What I liked best about this story is that these young men, then grown men, were able to sustain long, enduring friendships. This happens with women, but is rare for men."

— *Kyla Braun*, *survivor of suicide loss*

What others have said . . .

". . . moving, beautifully written, powerful: An unforgettable book."

— **_Kathleen Hall Jamieson, Ph.D._**, _award-winning author,_
professor of communication, Director, Annenberg Public Policy Center,
University of Pennsylvania

"Powerful. Vulnerable. Meaningful. I'm blown away by your authentic, heart-rending story... your confession, your love song. It will touch and help many."

— **_Tom Harrison_**, _former president/CEO, Russ Reid Company,_
the largest direct response fundraising firm in the U.S.

". . . it is the gist of these conversations among the sons that uncovers the terrible fallout of suicide – what those left behind struggle to deal with. If nothing else, this book illustrates the strength and power of the human spirit as the four of you connected and formed an invaluable therapy group."

— **_Bill Shumard_**, _president/CEO, Special Olympics Southern California_

". . . a profoundly moving account presented in a unique way. The courage demonstrated by the four of you will inspire others who share similar experiences. Beyond those for whom suicide of a parent is the reality, there are many more who have been touched, more or less directly, by suicide. They, too, will find understanding and even solace in your words."

— **_Stephen C. Wood, Ph.D._**, _professor of communication, University of Rhode Island_

"I gained a new understanding of what long-term, true friendship really means."

"This book will touch the hearts of those dealing not just with suicide but with any deeply felt child/parent challenges... which is probably many, many people."

— **_Bruce Burtch_**, _author, Win-Win for the Greater Good_

"I just finished reading *Sons of Suicide*. Wow. Like each of you said, there are no answers. But having that bond among this special group of friends makes all the difference. I was particularly touched reading the ongoing dialogue you all had through e-mails – so revealing and poignant."

— **Harold Rudnick**, *retired senior vice president, Vons Grocery Company*

". . . one of the best things I've ever read. It's powerful – much more than 'men spilling their guts.'"

— **Betty Vandermause**, *president, Merit Real Estate Analysis*

". . . compliments on the beautiful way you described the friendship among the four of you. I felt the story was even more about the importance of true friendship than the emotions exposed by a parent's suicide."

—**Jenny Mahoney**, *wife of Tom, one of the sons of suicide*

Table of Contents

Dedication

. . . .

To the memory of
Gloria Bernice Butensky Pincus
and
Dorothy Estelle Lipkin Knapp.
We wish we understood.

To all survivors of suicide loss.
You are not alone.

To the power of true friendship.
*For us it made **the** difference.*

"Life can only be understood backwards

but it must be lived forwards."

— *Søren Kierkegaard*

Prologue

....

The Healing Power
of Friendship

....

David—

Although I've only known you for three months, it seems like I've known you for years. You and I have so much in common, we could be brothers. In some ways, I feel we are.

Remember you always have a friend. Good luck at Long Beach State. Be sure to keep in touch and let me know when you're coming back.

Shalom,

Rick

—DuVal High School Yearbook, 1966

This is our story.

A story of two boys – now men, now fathers, now grandfathers.

A story of life-long friendship borne of life-shattering loss. A friendship so rare, so exquisitely timed, it initially saved us. And now helps sustain us.

A story of emotional struggles about men, told frankly and publicly by men – a rare, out-of-character telling by our gender, we've been told.

A story we've kept to ourselves for most of our lives.

We share it now knowing that too many others have been, or at some point will be, forced to endure an event as traumatic or even worse than the one we did.

We hope our story helps others realize they are not alone and that sharing their pain with someone they trust can lift at least some of their burden.

This story, we believe, isn't only *our* story.

— Rick & David

Chapter I

....

August, 1961
October, 1963

....

Brooklyn, NY

. . . .

My mother killed herself. *Two weeks after my 13th birthday.*

She had attempted suicide several times before. On two of those occasions, I witnessed snippets of the aftermath. Terrifying images are seared into my memory: My father breaking down the front door to our house after she swallowed a bottle of pills. Puddles of bright red blood on the bathroom floor after she slashed her wrists.

On the morning of her death, from the time I opened my eyes, a menacing feeling nagged at me. I'd never experienced such a strange feeling before, nor have I again. Before that day ended, I would realize it was warning me that something terrible had happened. Something that was about to change me – and life as I knew it – in ways I couldn't possibly imagine.

For years after her death, I felt lost and abandoned, aimless, alone. With nobody to talk to who had even an inkling of what it is like to be left behind that way.

Until a dreary March morning in Maryland almost five years later.

— David

Dayton, OH

. . . .

*M*y mother killed herself. I was 14. She was one week shy of her 40th birthday.

My sister and I waited in the car in the garage next to the downtown hotel where Mom had taken what Dad referred to as a short "vacation." Dad went in to get her, leaving us in the white Rambler station wagon. But for the longest time, neither of them showed up. I kept my sister occupied. We talked, told stories, played games. A stranger suddenly appeared and told us Dad would be with us shortly. More time passed. My nerves signaled something was terribly wrong, but I dutifully tried to keep my sister – and my mind – occupied.

When I finally saw Dad walk down the sloped floor of the garage, his head bowed, our rabbi was inexplicably by his side. Seconds later, I broke into tears.

For several years after Mom died, I felt trapped in a dense fog. I was vaguely aware of activity and events around me, some in slow motion, others at triple speed. My sister, brother and I – and our father – had no extended family around us and few friends, none of them particularly close. I felt alone.

Until a dreary March morning in Maryland almost three years later.

— Rick

Chapter II

....

September, mid-'90s

....

Cleveland, OH

. . . .

"**W**hen you think about your Mom these days, JD, what do you *think* . . . and *feel?*"

Rick utters the words with a nonchalance that defies the seriousness underlying the question. The same question we've been asking ourselves – and each other – since we met in the waning days of high school in March of 1966.

David, or JD (short for Joseph David) as Rick is prone to call him, gives his close friend of 30 years a curious stare and holds it for several beats.

"Where did *that* come from, Dickie?" Dickie is among a host of endearing (and not so endearing) nicknames David hatched for Rick years ago.

The mid-September air is heavy with heat and humidity. We are sitting on a thick wood-slatted bench on the grounds of Suburban Temple-Kol Ami, a Reform Jewish synagogue on the outskirts of Cleveland, taking a break from the Yom Kippur service. Translated as "The Day of Atonement," Yom Kippur is the holiest day of the Jewish year. It's when Jews seek forgiveness from the Almighty for their sins of the past year. As penance for trespasses committed and an uncomfortable reminder to live a holier life, "good" Jews fast for 24 hours to cleanse their bodies and souls.

We are trying to be good Jews, donning yarmulkes and being faithful to the High Holy Day for the full 24 hours, or as much of it as our constitutions will allow. Sundown is still five hours away and only then can the fast be "officially" broken. Our stomachs are already growling.

"I don't know." Rick resorts to a throwaway phrase to buy time to crystallize his thoughts. "The prayer of remembrance we said in temple today . . ."

"*Yizkor,*" David cuts in.

". . . well, it got me thinking about my mother, and your mother. It's been a while since we talked about them."

for worse, who knows for sure – just about everything important in my life . . . then and later. *Everything.*"

"Yeah, I know," Rick nods, signaling his understanding of David's situation – and his own. "After *my* mother died, nothing was ever the same again. But here's the thing I keep asking myself: Was that a good thing or a bad thing? Should I be thanking my mother for saving me from what my life would've been if she had lived as the unhappy person she was? Or should I be angry at her for denying me her presence in my life, regardless of how distressed she was in hers?"

"I've asked myself the very same questions," says David, sitting up ramrod straight, "more times than I can count."

"And?"

"And . . ." David gazes absent-mindedly at the ground. ". . . and I'm no closer to an answer I can live with today than the day she died." He half-turns toward Rick, whose kindhearted eyes are glued to him. "You?"

Rick shrugs. "Yes. No. Maybe. Depends on when I ask myself."

Almost in unison, we fold our arms into pretzel shapes over our chests and cross our legs at the ankles.

For the longest time, neither of us moves or utters a word, losing ourselves – each in his own way – in the muddy waters where we go when trying to make sense of the confusing circumstances that sealed our mothers' fates and tainted our memories of them.

• • • • • • • • • • • • • • • •

"Maybe we should go back in and pray for better answers," says Rick after a short break, pointing a thumb toward the synagogue.

"Probably should . . . since I understand God takes attendance today."

But neither of us makes a move to leave our bench; we know there is more to say.

"Let's get back to the original question," Rick insists, enunciating each syllable. "How did your life change after your mother ended her life?"

David lets out a long sigh of resignation. Talking about the shaky aftermath of his mother's senseless death never gets easier. "For one thing . . ." he slaps Rick on the knee, prompting him to look straight at David, "I wouldn't have come to live with my aunt and uncle in Maryland. And if that doesn't happen, ol' buddy, you and I never meet. The same goes for Karen, because I never would've gone to the University of Maryland. And without Karen, Jeffrey and Megan never exist, nor do my grandchildren, and on and on the story goes, all because my mother convinced herself we'd all be better off without her."

Slightly winded, David presses a palm on his thumping chest. As his breathing slows, blotches of sweat dot the front and back of his white button-down shirt.

"So, I guess what I'm saying," David says, "is that if not for our mothers' deaths, we're not sitting on this bench on this Yom Kippur having this conversation about destiny, coincidence, luck, misfortune, tragedy, comedy and what would've been or not been if this *one thing* – this one act of desperation – hadn't happened."

"Feels like we just took a trip back in time," Rick says as his eyes close, his voice trailing off to a whisper, "to when we first met in Bowie and . . ."

We sit still in the relative quiet of the moment, each considering the notion of destiny.

. . . .

"You know," Rick says with a straight face after a while, "you still haven't told me the biggest, juiciest sins you're atoning for. It's not too late. Let's hear 'em."

David thinks for a moment. Then, with an equally blank expression, says, "I would, but . . . we don't have nearly enough time for me to list them all."

We share a laugh and are about to stand when David stops. "Wait a minute," he says. "I know we're tired and hungry" – as if cued, his stomach lets out a loud grumble, sparking an exchange of boyish grins – "but now it's my turn to ask. How do you think the course of your life changed after your mom's death?" He waits for Rick to look at him. "What do you wonder about, Dickie?"

"Oh, I don't know." Rick settles back on the bench. "I know things would have been different. How could they not? But who knows how? Like you, I know there are ripple effects, some anticipated, others not . . . much like tossing a pebble into a still pond."

Rick is pensive, which ages him for an instant. David's eyes never leave his friend's face, the seconds ticking by.

"Maybe Dad never moves us from Ohio to Maryland," Rick restarts, leaning into David, their shoulders touching lightly. "Which means *I* never cross paths with *you.* Or I wind up in Maryland but our conversations only touch on routine stuff, like school and sports and politics."

"Don't forget girls."

"Never," Rick says, smiling half-heartedly, his thoughts a step ahead of his words. "Or," he peers straight at David, who's staring into the distance, "maybe we would have met but drifted apart after graduation, as we did with other buddies from those high school days."

"Now that's a scary thought," says David, glancing sideways at Rick.

Rick continues: "I've never stopped speculating how things might've been different – better? – if Mom had lived and my sister didn't have to grow up with a selfish, self-absorbed stepmother. I know living in that home environment was even harder for her than for me."

"It couldn't have been healthy for her," David shoots back a little too quickly, instantly wishing he could erase his words before they make Rick feel worse. Eyes closed, he shakes his head at himself. "Have you talked with her about all this?"

"Yes, though not much recently," Rick admits. "She's said many times she grew up without a positive female role model. Dad wasn't equipped to help a young pre-teen girl and teenager develop. And she feels Dad often treated her as if she were the adult woman in the house. He talked with her about his failing relationship with his wife. I don't think that's something a father would normally talk about with his daughter. He should have been talking with a counselor about those things."

"Hmmm," David nods, considering his next words carefully. "Your dad always struck me as the reserved type, who kept his emotions bottled up inside. Did he ever open up with you and your siblings about his life with your mom? About her death?"

Rick's expression turns sullen and he withdraws momentarily into a cocoon of silence that seems to say, "Don't push me." After a minute or two, David homes in on the strained relationship we prefer to avoid: our fathers.

"After your mom died, did you and your dad grow closer or drift further apart?"

It is one of those nagging, impenetrable questions that is always pertinent and always frustrating. For both of us. Though David posed the question, it applies as much to him. Just as questions surrounding our mothers' deaths transformed us as individuals, sons, siblings, spouses, fathers, grandfathers and friends. Though we are rarely satisfied or comforted by our answers, the honest sharing of thoughts and feelings, fears and regrets, hopes and dreams, is what led us into, and keeps us in, this uncommon friendship.

"Dad was stoic – and that's an understatement. He never really talked about Mom's suicide. It's not even a word he would've used. For a long time, things with Dad were awkward, distant . . . and absent genuine emotions, at least outwardly," Rick says, his chin dipping toward his chest.

"Yeah, I know." David squeezes Rick's shoulder and holds it. "Mine, too."

. . . .

Not surprisingly, we don't make it back to Temple-Kol Ami for the breaking of the fast.

For the next hour, we remain fixed to that hard bench in the sweltering heat, growing hungrier and thirstier, and drawing closer as kindred spirits. Closer than we had in a long time.

In a way, looking back on that day now we see its meaning more clearly, understand its impact more fully. We presided over our own High Holy Day service, a spirited and spiritual one, not in the somber atmosphere of a synagogue mumbling prayers we barely understood, but outside on a splintery wood bench rehashing dense questions we'll never resolve and anguished memories we'll never forget.

The very same questions and memories that first drew us to one another 30 years earlier . . .

Chapter III

....

March, 1966

....

Bowie, MD

· ·

The two of us meet by happenstance on a street corner in Bowie, Maryland.

Our memories of that dreary March morning more than 50 years ago are remarkably similar.

We are both 17-year-old high school seniors, though Rick is half a year younger and never lets David forget that fact. Rick has returned to Maryland from six months in Hawaii where his father had a temporary assignment. He is waiting for the school bus on the wrong corner of the intersection and David, with a mix of disdain and generosity, hails him from across the street.

"Hey, you goin' to DuVal?" David shouts. Rick had arrived early to the spot where he'd been told to catch the bus and watched dubiously as a cluster of teenagers gradually gathered on the opposite corner.

It is our first interaction, and neither of us has the slightest hunch how fortuitous this chance meeting would turn out to be.

"Yeah," Rick shouts back.

"Over here," David signals him to cross the street.

We can't recall whether we talked much on the bus ride to school that day, or just when our conversations became more than perfunctory. But we know it happened quickly.

Within a matter of days – maybe a week – we begin discovering how much we have in common. We were both born in New York City, although David lived there through part of his childhood and Rick did not, and both still have family there. Baseball was – and remains – our favorite sport; David is a Dodgers fan given his Brooklyn roots and Rick pulls for the Dodgers' long-time archrivals, the Yankees, given his Manhattan origins (across the river from the Bronx). Both of us are Jewish. Throughout our childhoods and our teen years, we each moved often, living in multiple cities in multiple states.

And, as we are about to learn, we both are sons of suicide.

. . . .

Putting into words the essence of a close friendship – a deep, abiding relationship – is next to impossible.

Perhaps it's better that way, so as not to spoil the mystique.

Or maybe Henry David Thoreau had the right idea when he wrote, "The language of friendship is not words, but meanings."

Talk about meanings. In our case, it has now been five decades since we stumbled into *the* conversation that initially shocked us, later drew us together, and eventually shepherded us into a life-long, unbreakable friendship.

. . . .

"Why is it you're living with your aunt and uncle and not your father and moth – uh, I mean stepmother in Brooklyn?" Rick asks.

"Step . . . mother?" David shakes his head, as if trying to erase the word from his memory. "Never thought of her in any terms with 'mother' in it."

It is after school and only a week or two since we stumbled upon one another at the bus stop. We still are in the "getting to know you" phase. Until now, we had managed to avoid anything too personal or controversial; school, sports, college plans, pretty girls was about the extent of any conversation.

David can't hide his discomfort. He sits on one end of the couch that stretches along the outer wall of his makeshift bedroom. He rearranges himself as he considers the far-reaching, unbearably complicated question, one fraught with a bevy of knotty implications, most of which he'd rather not touch just yet. Rick faces him from the other end of the couch.

Though Rick's question seems simple enough, David doesn't have a quick or simple answer. There's too much warped history to try to explain, much of it muddled by complications and qualifications.

Rick waits, displaying an innate patience David would come to envy. David studies his new friend as he weighs the upside and downside of opening the Pandora's Box concealing his splintered life. He knows that once opened, its contents can't ever be returned.

"I had no place else to go, so…" David mutters finally. "I was supposed to go live with my grandmother in her teeny condo in Miami Beach. My mother's mother. But that would've been a disaster. Everybody but my grandmother knew it. But as fate would have it, that's when Aunt and Unc opened their door to me."

"But why not live with your dad?"

Why, indeed, David thinks. How to explain in a few words a situation so convoluted, so dysfunctional, he could hardly explain it to himself.

"Well, he, uh… His wife, they didn't…"

David stops himself and squeezes his eyes shut, wishing he could somehow purge from his memory the nauseating four words that altered his destiny and have shadowed him with the doggedness of a bill collector ever since.

"He told me that, uh… *the door is closed.*"

Those were his father's exact words – words carved deep into David's memory… and his soul.

He never asked his father why he said them or if he really meant them, but deep down he knew, even if it would be years before he could admit it to himself. He was obsessed with escaping from his preoccupied father and the insincere and scheming woman (with three children) his father married less than a year after the funeral of David's mother. As a result, David had become a behavioral handful his father didn't want jeopardizing his new marriage. Whether closing the door to him was his father's or the wife's decision (David always sensed her indifference to him and his sister), or theirs together, it hardly mattered. The net effect on his deteriorating relationship with his father – which never got much better – would have been the same either way. David came to believe that his father convinced himself he had little choice other than to do whatever he thought necessary to preserve his second marriage, even if it meant sacrificing one or both of his children.

"Do you think he meant it *literally?*" Already a budding journalist, Rick probes gently, coaxing David to reveal more. "Seems pretty harsh. Maybe he was showing off in front of his new wife."

David shoots Rick an unmistakable "are you kidding me?" stare. He is neither ready, nor willing, to go down this road any farther with a guy he doesn't yet trust. Plus, it's still an open wound that stings like crazy. As hard as he tries to ignore it, there is something about Rick's temperament – his genuineness maybe, or his mellow, unguarded manner – luring David from the false safety of his silence.

"I'm not living with him... or her ... or her kids... am I?" he spits out the words.

"No... you... are... not." Rick mirrors David's exaggerated cadence.

Rick, of course, understands the inherently thorny, clashing nature of the father-son relationship. Even so, he's unable to comprehend how that relationship could unravel to the point of such desperation that a father would willingly cast aside his 17-year-old son. Realizing he and David don't know each other well enough yet for that discussion, Rick lets it go for another day. Besides, he is actually more interested in a different question. A question that, though he couldn't know it then, would soon change both their lives in meaningful and lasting ways.

"Where's your *real* mom?"

Neither of us ever welcomes that bombshell question – certainly not back then but even now, half a century later. In 1966, a few years after our mothers' suicides, we were still reeling and confused about the flurry of events that decimated our families, leaving us to try to figure out on our own where, in the debris, we belonged. A far easier strategy than trying to explain the mess was simply to sidestep the question altogether.

"She's gone."

David's discomfort is instantly apparent, and he clams up. So Rick prods him, mildly at first. "Gone? Meaning living somewhere else? Or gone, meaning..."

At this point, we both remain wary, cautious, and sensitive to opening ourselves to the risks of allowing someone we don't yet trust or even know all that well into our bruised inner sanctums.

"Yeah. She's dead."

"When?"

"Almost five years ago." Then, as if remembering for the first time in a long time, he adds, "Two weeks to the day after I turned 13."

"Tough time." Rick peers at David through eyes filling with empathy. "I lost my mom when I was 14."

David hesitates. Experience tells him that if he poses the next logical question, he'll be asked it in return. Which he doesn't want in the worst way. Neither does Rick, he presumes. So, to spare both of them for now, he resorts to a bit of misdirection.

"What was your mom's name?"

Caught off-guard, Rick squints warily at David – and his oddly timed question. "Her name? You wanna know her name?" David just nods, as Rick studies him hard, trying to catch sight of what makes this guy tick.

"Dorothy," he says guardedly, leaning in just a bit.

David smiles to himself, and says, "Over the rainbow . . . Oz."

Amused by the off-hand quip, Rick can't hold off a small smile himself. "Yeah," he mutters under his breath, "over the rainbow." The somber mood that had been building lightens. "And your's name?"

David looks away as he mumbles, "Gloria."

Rick considers the name. "*In excelsis Deo* . . . Christmas song."

Out of the corner of his eye, he catches David fighting back the beginnings of a grin. Touché!

Rick says nothing as he ponders whether to pose the dreaded, inevitable question now or later. Then he hears a voice – not his own – speak the very words he was about to say.

"How did she . . . die?" David's halting half-whisper is barely audible in the quiet of the closed off second-floor room.

The lightning rod question. And even though we're now more adept at camouflaging our emotions when the topic arises, merely hearing the word – *suicide* – still feels like a stiff jab to the heart.

"Suicide."

Almost before the word is out of his mouth, Rick appears exhausted, emotionally depleted.

David's eyes bulge, his face freezes. "No . . . no," he offers suspiciously. "I don't believe it." He wants to believe it, selfishly. But he can't stop himself from thinking he's dreaming this or is the unwitting victim of a twisted ruse.

Equally confounded, Rick whispers in a raspy voice choked with emotion, "Your's too?" He doesn't mean it as a question.

"Mine, too." David readjusts himself on the narrow couch so he's facing Rick squarely.

In that unlikely moment, we both remember thinking, "How could this be?" We had met only days before, purely by accident. Yet here we are – same age, same religion, same interests, same home town – and we've both experienced the same incomprehensible loss of a parent by suicide at about the same point in our lives?

"Suicide?" Rick asks, needing verification.

"Suicide," murmurs David, who still claims that saying the despised word is akin to chewing a mouthful of broken glass.

"How?"

David looks away, his gaze drifting through the window above the couch to rows of grassy backyards crammed with rusting barbecues, assorted gardening tools, bicycles of all sizes, and an occasional hammock.

He pinches the bridge of his nose, fighting back emotions beginning to overtake him.

"Pills." His raised eyebrows pose the same question to Rick.

"Same."

"Really?"

"Uh-huh. And probably some booze."

In that moment of awakening, a door between us is pushed open.

"Had she tried before?" Rick asks reluctantly, skirting eye contact.

David's reflex is to pull back and avoid this discussion at all costs, but for some reason he doesn't. "Yeah. At least two other times I know of . . . But I've been told she tried several other times, going back to when she was around our age."

We stare helplessly at one another, trying to absorb so much at once.

"I think it was Mom's first time," Rick says, his mood turning darker. "And the last," he adds unnecessarily.

David studies Rick's face and body, then asks, "What was she like, your mom? You know . . . when she was feeling herself?" The question, one seldom asked of those closest to suicide victims, momentarily disarms Rick. Bit by bit, warmth spreads across his face. He's sensitive to the implicit compassion rooted in the asking.

"She was sweet and kind, sometimes. I have some good memories . . ."

"Such as?" David insists when a pensive Rick hesitates, appearing to have gotten sidetracked rummaging among memories of his mother.

Then, as if coming out of a trance, he's back. "I can remember Mom sitting on Dad's lap in the living room and the two of them slow-dancing to a Sinatra song in the kitchen. I remember resting my arms on her shoulders – we were both standing, but as short as I am, she was even shorter by the time I was 11 or 12. It was sort of a special hug the two of us shared.

"For the most part, Dad was the disciplinarian when I was a kid. But I remember Mom taking a hairbrush to my backside for something I did. I probably deserved it. And one time, she caught me playing with matches. So she sat me down at the kitchen table and handed me a box of matches. Then she made me light every one. And she made me hold the burning match until the flame touched my fingertips. Then I could drop it into a coffee can that had a couple inches of water in it. I didn't play with matches again, I'll tell you that!"

Rick pauses, his soft smile slowly giving way to a somber expression.

"I also remember her seeming at wit's end at times. I have a mental picture of her being panicked when I came in red-faced and sweaty after riding my bike around the neighborhood on a hot summer day. She was clearly worried that I had done something terrible to myself. And another time, the summer before she died, when I staggered into the house with my first-ever migraine headache. I'd ridden the bus home after caddying at a local country club. I could barely see. My head was pounding. I was nauseous and disoriented. And neither of us had any idea what was happening. She put a cold washcloth on my forehead. She had me sit for a while then took me to lie down. I'm not sure how soon afterward, but I was tested in the hospital – an EEG with pins stuck in my scalp – to see if there was some kind of tumor or if I'd had a stroke, I guess.

"I do remember times when Mom was sad. Or maybe distressed. Or lonely. All the rest of the family was back in New York. And she didn't have many friends that I remember. That's how she seemed to me, anyway. But, truthfully . . ."

Rick suddenly breaks eye contact with David, clearly disturbed by a troubling memory or thought.

"Since it happened, though . . ." he focuses on his tightly intertwined hands, "I've been wondering if I ever knew the real her."

"I get that," David nods vigorously. "When I think of my mother now, I see her stretched out on the living room couch, wracked by a bad back, looking terribly unhappy and waiting for, uh, waiting for I don't know what . . . death, maybe."

Looking up, startled, David is affected by his own words – words he has never thought, much less said out loud. "But there were also times when she was all smiles, so beautiful to look at, seemingly free of all her troubles. That's the mother I so wish I could remember. Those smiling times weren't often, and they never lasted very long. I used to think of her as a Jekyll and Hyde who wasn't sure which one she wanted to be."

· · · · · · · · · · · · · · · ·

What are the odds that the two of us – or any two individuals who share the exact same tragic loss at practically the same age – cross paths in our lifetimes? Just coincidence? Just luck? Or something more cosmic at work?

In the days and weeks that follow, we pour out our life stories, revealing fragments of our souls to each other – and to ourselves – with a raw, urgent honesty we'd been unable to summon with anyone else. We are eager to express pent up emotions, and the conversations could take place anywhere: During after-school walks home from the bus stop, holed up in our bedrooms, or plunked on our favorite bench in Fox Hill Park midway between our homes.

Looking back now at those momentous few weeks after we met, we quickly went from strangers to friends . . . then from friends to brothers. Our friendship, which salvaged two teenagers struggling to make sense of death and life, has endured and flourished these many decades. Neither of us can imagine our lives without the other in it.

. . . .

Expressing the emotional relief we each feel after discovering that we're both struggling to come to terms with our mothers' suicides is near-impossible.

After school, we walk the mile from the bus stop to Rick's house or, more often, the couple of blocks to David's place where "our" Aunt Phyllis welcomes us home with milk and Oreos. Our conversations range far and wide, from classes to sports to college ambitions, yet we almost always wend our way back to rehashing the days leading up to the shock of our mothers' deaths and the brutal aftermath when our lives ruptured.

Bowie is a Levitt community of tract homes built in the late 1950s and '60s. William Levitt was famous for his developments of nice homes, typically five or so models that could be built quickly at moderate cost. Aunt Phyllis and Uncle Ben live in a two-story colonial on Kayhill Lane, white with light turquoise shutters and a covered front porch. A thriving weeping willow encompasses almost the entire front lawn.

David, estranged from his father after the suicide and unable to accept his father's quick remarriage, had moved in with his mother's closest friend and her family in

California for two of his high school years. But by the end of those two years, he couldn't ignore his yearning to be with his own family again. So, at their invitation, he went to his aunt and uncle's Maryland home for his senior year. Phyllis, Ben and their two young daughters welcomed him as if he were their own son and brother.

Ben, a Navy veteran and civilian engineer who works for the Department of the Navy, has an analytic mind, along with a quick and sometimes quirky sense of humor. He is known for playing tricks on unwitting subjects. One night, when Phyllis has invited Rick to stay for dinner, Ben deliberately positions himself at the table to Rick's right. Plates are filled and distributed. Ben begins regaling the group with one of his stories. As Rick starts bringing a forkful of food toward his mouth, Ben diverts his attention by over-emphasizing whatever point he is making while gently but firmly pressing a finger on Rick's forearm, preventing him from eating. Oblivious to what's happening, Rick again lifts his fork to his mouth and once more Ben, talking all the while and forcing eye contact with his hungry mark, repeats the subtle maneuver. Still unaware of his featured role in the ruse, Rick hoists his fork toward his mouth a third time – and again is thwarted.

By now, neither David nor his cousins can keep a straight face. And Rick, yet to have gotten a bite of dinner, finally realizes he's the brunt of Uncle Ben's practical joke and leads the laughter that follows.

Aunt Phyllis exudes casual elegance, warmth and kindness. She is David's father's sister, though the siblings' personalities and outlooks on life are poles apart. Phyllis is a homemaker in the truest sense – the heart and soul of the family, an extraordinary role model for her daughters and an inspiration for others. To her, genuinely caring for those close to her and those close to them is as natural as blinking. The fact that she and Ben opened their home to David at a critical juncture in his life was emblematic of their generosity, empathy and open-heartedness. A genuine caring that naturally extended to David's new pal, Rick, from the start. David's Aunt and "Unc" became Rick's, too.

A 20-minute walk away, on Lerner Place, Rick lives in a four-bedroom, story-and-a-half house with his father, stepmother, younger sister, and older brother who had transferred to the University of Maryland at their father's insistence so the family would be together in their new home. Like David's Uncle Ben, Rick's dad, Mark, is an engineer and a World War II vet. He now assists the Defense Department, NASA and other organizations through an independent research think-tank. Mark's approach to life is even more analytical than Ben's. Although he could sometimes toss back his head in unabashed laughter, he is not naturally spontaneous except for the occasional display of anger. He is often stern and judgmental. Still, Mark clearly has an affinity for David and enjoys watching the two teenagers grow closer as their friendship develops.

Rick's home life is made more difficult by the contentious relationship he and his siblings (and soon his father) have with his stepmother. She is often irrational, especially in her attempts to exercise her new-found authority as a stepparent.

The challenging relationships we have with our fathers and their wives (our *step*mothers) only serves to fortify the connection between us and, along with our mothers' suicides, are subjects of intense discussion on walks between our houses after school, or hanging out on our favorite bench in Fox Hill Park, up the street from Rick's house. As befit the vernacular of the mid-'60s, we quickly began referring to these heart-to-heart conversations as "soul sessions." Before long, we had our own shorthand for them. "How 'bout an SS?"

Most adolescents struggle with the Big Questions of life, trying to define themselves as independent adults and redefine their relationships with parents, coping with changing hormones, wondering about the mysteries of the opposite sex. Yes, we grappled with these topics. But our soul sessions tended toward weightier life issues. Punctuated, of course, with rambunctious debates about matters crucial to humanity, like whether Willie Mays was a better centerfielder than Mickey Mantle and Duke Snider. The conversations invariably circled back to our mothers' plights and deaths, and our determined efforts to understand what drove them to give up on life and how to survive the messed up home lives they bequeathed us.

Each soul session covered familiar ground and simultaneously unearthed new territory. This would be true even years later. As much as the two of us know about each other, we learn something new and gain fresh insight with each conversation. After a while, as trust solidified, no topic was prohibited or left unexplored between us.

High school graduation was anticlimactic for both of us – a virtual non-event. Our graduating class numbered well over 900, and neither of us had spent more than a small portion of our high school days at DuVal. David was there only as a senior; Rick for his junior year and the last few months of high school.

The hectic summer after high school, between working and readying for college life, passed in a flash. Before we knew it, we were saying good-bye as David switched coasts to begin a new adventure at Cal State Long Beach while Rick remained close to home and his younger sister, enrolling at the University of Maryland.

Soul sessions were relegated – for the time being – to occasional letters and hurried phone calls.

Chapter IV

....

August, 2009

....

McCormick & Schmick's, Chicago, IL

· ·

Fast forward more than 40 years.

Chicago.

We all feel compelled to be there. This is a gathering years in the making.

The two of us – David and Rick – sit across from each other in the restaurant booth. Dennis[1] and Tom slide in next to us on the brown and tan banquettes. The discussion is somber, though punctuated by lighter moments of teasing and laughter. One of the four talks, the rest listening in rapt attention, oblivious to the chatter at adjacent tables or the din trying to impose itself from the bar. The subject is deeply personal, the emotions still raw, even decades after the events that prompted them. If one of us pauses for a few seconds, hunting for the right words to express himself – or needing a moment to clear the lump in his throat – the others wait patiently, empathetically.

Some of what we disclose this night we have never told another soul – and some we have never been able to articulate, even to ourselves.

On this special occasion, our "soul session" has four participants instead of the usual two.

Hours pass as the four of us order drinks, then dinner, refusing to be hurried by an attentive waiter or constrained by the clock.

Condensation pools around the water glasses dotting the dark, highly lacquered wood table. Occasional questions lightly pepper what otherwise is a series of monologues recounting the most heartbreaking moment in each of our lives.

This foursome has never been together, face-to-face, until today. Chicago, a city easily accessible by air, is a logical location. David and Dennis arrived yesterday and shared some twosome time; Rick and Tom got in today. The four of us congregated

---

[1] At his request, "Dennis" is a pseudonym. Only his name and some identifiers have been changed.

at our hotel late this afternoon. After the usual niceties, we reviewed our plans for the next few days – a baseball game (Yankees vs. White Sox on the South Side), mandatory Chicago deep-dish pizza and, we decide on the spot, an architectural boat ride on the Chicago River. We discuss dinner options, and prefer staying close to the hotel for our long-awaited first evening all together. McCormick & Schmick's, an upscale classic seafood and steak restaurant, is chosen because of its proximity, reputation and conversation-friendly ambience.

The Friday night crowd has filled the place. A mix of luscious aromas encircles us, stoking our appetites.

"*L'chaim,*" David toasts, eyes beaming as four glasses are raised in unison and clink together as one. "To life . . . and friendship," he adds in a voice wavering with emotion, and repeats the words as he gazes into the faces of his three friends.

Sipping his champagne cocktail, David, who drinks almost no alcohol, immediately declares that the tip of his nose is already numb. Rick nurses a single-malt Glenfiddich, neat with a twist of lemon. Tom starts on his first Black Russian. Dennis lets the head on his Bass Ale subside before tasting it, then licks his lips in obvious approval.

Like the rest of us, Dennis is "middle age" – if we each live to be 110 or so. His demeanor is quiet, thoughtful and understated; he is tall, trim and looks younger than his years. David and Dennis met in passing in their professional lives years ago in Southern California, but didn't strike up a relationship until after they both relocated elsewhere (Arkansas, Colorado); once they realized the mix of interests they shared, acquaintanceship soon morphed into friendship. A talented writer and photographer, Dennis now freelances travel articles for newspapers and magazines. He and his wife, Mary, a British import, are avid travelers and hikers and enjoy a rich social life in Boulder.

We've known Tom much longer, dating back to the late 1970s. Although we met him in the Washington, D.C., area as fellow communication professionals (coincidentally, through a chapter of the same association in which David and Dennis met), he has since retired to New Zealand with his wife, Jen, who has family there. They return to the States each summer for a few months to be with their American family and friends. The oldest member of the dinner group by a few years, Tom was a broadcast journalist with National Public Radio and, later, the Voice of America. When we first encountered Tom, he was working in corporate public relations at AT&T; Rick later became a manager there.

Befitting his profession, Tom's melodic deep baritone can be mesmerizing. A skilled writer with a wide-ranging, expressive vocabulary, he thrives on pontificating about injustices in the world – particularly the malfunctions and malfeasances of American politics and government. He rarely appears to be in a hurry; he savors conversation, and good food and drink, not necessarily in that order. That could be problematic on other occasions, but on this evening, there is no sense of urgency, no schedule to keep, and all of us are fully engaged, captivated by the long-awaited group gathering.

The discussion is a deeply personal continuation of one started several years earlier in an unplanned email exchange that built in intensity over several weeks.

David prompted that electronic back-and-forth with a simple email query seeking help for a writing project he had in mind, knowing that we *four* are, inescapably, sons of suicide . . .

Chapter V

······································

April 27-28, 2005

······································

From: **David**
To: Dennis, Rick, Tom
Subject: *Sharing of Like Souls*
Date: April 27, 2005

Rick, Tom and Dennis —

I know two of you only know the third (Dennis) through me, but by now you are aware of the heartbreak we four share: the suicide of a parent.

I have a favor to ask. A favor requiring you to dig deep within yourself.

What I'm asking is, in one regard, merely research help for a fictional story I'm planning to write, but it may actually be much more. I'm asking you to share memories from one of, if not the, most emotionally grueling time in your life.[2]

My hope is that you'll want to participate, in part to enlighten me as a writer about "our" story, but also, perhaps, to "unburden" yourself of some of the hefty emotional baggage we all still carry. I know of the powerful pull not to talk about this terrible time in your life; for me, it had always been a case of lockjaw until the three of you came into my life. Talking with you about my mother's shocking end got easier, because you understand instantly and so much less need be explained.

I *think* I know my own feelings and beliefs regarding the impact of a parent's suicide on the children left behind. But are my perceptions typical or unusual? In writing this story, I'm not willing to rely solely on my own experience. This is why I need your help.

Here are a few questions to help start your mental and emotional engines. Whatever you care to say, and however you choose to express it, will be welcome and very much appreciated . . .

- What were the dominant emotions you felt at the time of your parent's suicide, and how did those feelings change, and change you, over the years?

---

[2] David's original plan for a novel was eventually abandoned in favor of this memoir. The emails interspersed among the narrative scenes are comprised of the actual emails we four wrote on the dates noted, with a few select additions for explanatory purposes, and edited for brevity and clarity only.

- To what extent did you understand why your parent took his or her life? And did that understanding make it easier or harder for you to accept your parent's choice to end his or her life?

- How willing have you been to talk openly about your private thoughts and feelings? In who have you most often confided?

- How do you perceive your lost parent today, many years later, compared to the emotional whirlwind in the months and years following the suicide?

- How has that terrible singular event influenced the course of your life, decisions you've made, relationships you've won and lost, since then? How might things have been different had your parent chosen to live rather than die?

- To what extent do you feel tainted by your lost parent's suicide? Has that experience influenced how you see yourself and your likelihood to consider suicide?

I'm eager to hear whatever you're comfortable sharing. But if you're uncomfortable, that's okay too; I understand.

Thanks, friends – and brothers – for all you are and mean to me . . . David

From: Tom
To: David, Dennis, Rick
Subject: Re: Sharing of Like Souls
Date: April 28, 2005

Always good to hear from you, Davey, and learn why I have been in your thoughts recently.

Plus a long overdue hello to Rick (w/love to Ellen) and also to your friend, Dennis.

I'm about go out for groceries (Jenny's cracking the whip again!), but I wanted you to know I'll be happy to share my thoughts and feelings in the coming months about the important story you want to tell – one which has touched the lives of each of us.

We can "talk" via cyber-grams and phone calls, Davey, and must do a face-to-face chat or two when we visit the States – be it in Cleveland, Baltimore, Washington . . . or during a side trip to Arkansas.

I'll know more about travel plans within a week or so. Talk with you soon.

Best regards,

Tom

Chapter VI

....

June, 1999

....

Baseball Road Trip, Chicago, IL

. . . .

Tom's short note was the first response to David's query.

Remarkably, although Tom already had been Rick and David's colleague and close friend for some 20 years by now, we had no inkling that he was another "son" until the first stop on a baseball road trip.

The three of us are perched on a park bench, Tom in the middle, overlooking a shallow urban beach on the edge of Lake Michigan. The conversation starts innocuously enough, with a review of the trip so far and speculation about ballgames and ballparks still to come.

The green paint covering the wood bench is peeling and flaking, a victim of Chicago's famous wind, harsh winter and constant dampness coming off the lake. Though the sun is bright, the air has a slight chill and the three of us are wearing light jackets. Tom, long susceptible to pulmonary problems, has zipped his to the neck.

"Did you love being there, in that idyllic setting?" Rick asks Tom, referring to Hawaii where both once lived. Tom had been there on a military assignment; a few years later, Rick found himself in the Aloha State during the first seven months of his senior year of high school.

Tom half turns toward Rick to acknowledge the question, but is suddenly distracted, peering off into the distance as if in search of long-lost memories. "Yes, I loved it . . ." he mutters unconvincingly, ". . . until the two phone calls."

"Phone calls?" David takes the bait.

"Yeah," Tom says in his rich radio voice so easy on the ear. A wave of sadness overtakes him. "The second was from my first love telling me she was seeing another guy . . . and, and . . . she expected to become engaged to him soon."

This is new territory in our three-way relationship. More intimate, more revealing than any discussion we'd had before. So Tommy has our undivided attention.

He has opened a window into himself, however reluctantly. Choosing his words judiciously, he explains – as matter-of-factly as he can – how he and his first love had yielded to their parents' urging to abort a pregnancy neither of them was emotionally or financially prepared to take on. "With youthful naiveté," Tom says, the bittersweet reminiscence reflected in his gloomy stare, "we wanted to raise the baby ourselves." After the trauma of the abortion, despite their feelings for each other, their relationship began to crumble, and eventually collapsed.

Both of us pause to let Tom's revelation soak in, and to give him time to recover.

Our eyes wander to the shimmering swath of Lake Michigan stretching before us, and then beyond it, to the majestic, colossal Ferris wheel standing guard over Navy Pier.

. . . .

"That had to be a tough phone call to process when you're thousands of miles away. But you said two calls. What about the first one?"

David unknowingly steers Tom back down the rabbit hole to the most cataclysmic period of his life.

Tom begins haltingly, hunching forward, refusing to look at either of us. "It came from the military command in Hawaii. The news that . . . that Dad had, uh, taken his life . . . and they wanted to put me on a plane back to Rochester."

We shoot incredulous stares at each other, the startling admission catapulting us back in time to when, as needy, lonely 17-year-olds, we confided in one another the "secret" of our mothers' suicides. And here we are, hearing a close friend's horrific, heartbreaking testimony all over again.

Suddenly, in the blink of an eye, membership in our exclusive little club jumps from two to three. And a close friend becomes even closer.

Tom's eyes well up with tears – of sadness or relief, we can't tell – as he falls silent. Ironically, in this somber moment the only sounds to break that silence are children's happy voices floating on a light breeze wafting off the glimmering lake.

Softly, his voice tinged with compassion, Rick says, "We understand, Tom . . . far more than you know."

Tom throws a befuddled gaze toward Rick, imploring him to explain.

"How many years have the three of us known one another?" Rick isn't expecting a response, and he doesn't get one. "Yet somehow we've never talked about the parents we've lost." He steals another glance at David.

"Jeez, this can't be," David sputters, the words escaping on their own. "Not again."

"What can't be . . . *again*?" asks Tom, as his eyes jump from Rick to David and back to Rick again.

David nods for Rick to go on. "Our mothers, Tommy." Stopping himself, Rick peers at David, whose steely expression propels him forward. "They took their own lives, too. When we were barely teenagers."

"What?" Tom is flabbergasted, much as the two of us were 33 years ago. Which now seems more like 33 *minutes* ago.

"Yeah, we get it," Rick says, gripping Tom's shoulder. "Makes you wonder, doesn't it?"

Tom shakes his head over and over in disbelief. "How is it possible that this – something so important, so meaningful, so much a part of us . . . How could it be this never came up in the hundreds of talks we've had in all the years we've been friends? It's inconceivable."

"I'll second that," says David.

"And I'll third it," adds Rick.

· · · · · · · · · · · · · · · · ·

Suicide is the last topic we would have predicted arising during this "buddy" road trip. Chicago is the first stop on a three-city, four-ballpark baseball road trip of four long-time friends who share a passion for the game and its history – and a determination to experience Detroit's venerable Tiger Stadium in the last of its 87 historic seasons. After two games in Chicago – the Cubs at Wrigley, the White Sox at Comiskey – Detroit is next up before wrapping up with an Indians game at "The Jake" (Jacobs Field) in Cleveland, Rick's home base.

Our friend Mike, the fourth of our merry band of roadsters, had hot-footed it back to Maryland the day before to be at his youngest daughter's elementary school graduation; he will rejoin us tomorrow morning in time for the drive to Tiger Stadium. After David and Mike hit it off as fellow grad students at the University of Maryland in the early '70s, Mike – as amiable, good-natured and easygoing a guy as God ever created – soon struck up friendships with David's other close friends, beginning, of course, with Rick.

That the three of us are on *this* bench having *this* conversation at *this* precise moment seems otherworldly, unfathomable – something out of a Stephen King novel. Yet the truth is, if Mike hadn't skipped town for a few hours, leaving the three of us here to kill time, it's doubtful we would have had this conversation on *this* day. Or maybe ever.

"Suicide isn't exactly an everyday subject of conversation, is it?" says David, nudging Tom with an elbow, triggering the hint of a smile. "I can count the number of people I've talked to about my mother's suicide – ever – on both hands and still leave several fingers untouched."

"Why do you think your dad did it, Tom? Take his own life?" Rick asks, a reflex question that comes with club membership.

"I've asked myself that very question every day since it happened. And the inadequate answer never changes," Tom sighs, his exasperation unmistakable. "I know, or think I know, why he lost hope and why he couldn't face himself, or his family. Then, in the next minute, I'm not sure I have a clue why he did it. But God, I wish I did. Really knew. Like what he was thinking and feeling in that terrible split second when he decided to cut his wrists and let the life drain from his body… " – he gulps for air to steady himself – "…and our lives."

Staring at our still-stunned, perplexed friend, we feel his pain and confusion – as well as our own, once more. Like us, he's convinced himself that if he could just know *why* he would be magically freed of the anguish and frustration he's carried since the phone call informing him of his father's suicide.

"Did he care so little about me, my sister, Mom," Tom continues the monologue, his faltering voice growing in volume and intensity, "and the thousands of memories we had accumulated together over the years, to do *this*? To himself? To me? To us?"

Then, peering into the calm waters of Lake Michigan, he whispers so softly his words are barely audible, "Couldn't he see another way? Couldn't he..."

· · · · · · · · · · · · · · · · ·

A s Tom gathers himself, he begins describing his father's demons. Oddly, doing so seems to calm him, and bring him a trace of comfort.

"When and why his downward spiral began, I couldn't say. But I think I know some of the reasons why, late in his life, Dad was drawn toward suicide. He was a traveling salesman in the classic sense. Spent a lot of time on the road, smoked two packs of Camels a day, and consumed too much alcohol. Always an excellent driver – he taught me how – one night, while drunk, he caused a deadly crash that claimed the life of a driver in another car. He never recovered from the deep guilt that consumed him and robbed him of his self-esteem . . . and, ultimately, his desire to go on living.

"But after the car accident and from then on, his personality and behavior changed..." – he shakes his head several times, plainly bothered by whatever memories of his dad have surfaced in his mind's eye – ". . . and he became unpredictable, atypically quiet, undependable, uncaring. Pretty soon he withdrew into the bottle and dropped into his own inner hell. He'd disappear for weeks at a time, causing Mom endless worry and frustration as she tried to help Dad deal with his desire for self-destruction that was devouring him. Eventually, he had a nervous breakdown, spent time in a mental hospital, and became increasingly distant and depressed. He was never again the man I so deeply loved and admired growing up and who was my rock throughout most of my life until then."

Tom's body sags; he is emotionally and physically spent. But we can't let him stop now.

"How did you reconcile his death with your life, Tommy?" David asks.

"I'm not sure I have . . . or ever will." Tensing up, he seems upset, though with himself or his Dad, or both, we can't tell – and leave it alone.

"For years, I could hardly contain the anger raging inside me. Not long after I returned to Hawaii, I started experiencing bouts of depression and, uh –" He clears his throat a few times more than necessary, bracing himself for what he's about to admit. "On a couple of occasions I gave serious thought to following in Dad's footsteps. I was deeply troubled, and retreated inside my grief, shutting out others close to me, like the woman I thought I was going to marry, who reacted by pulling back because she didn't recognize me anymore."

"It still upsets me to think about him, which I hadn't done too often until fairly recently. But, if I'm honest with myself, I've managed to cut Dad some slack, I think. I'm talking about him more and that's brought back a flood of memories of the man I recall looking up to as a kid, and the many good times we shared before . . . before . . . before he . . . stopped believing in himself. Like the social person he was, his great sense of humor, and the many father-son times we spent together. In other words, I suppose I'd say that the initial anger that almost destroyed *me* has finally lost its iron grip on me and, mercifully, been replaced by a more objective perspective on the events that changed *him* and led to his tragic decision that not only ended his life but forever reshaped mine, my sister's and Mom's."

Then, as if summoned by some cosmic force, a light, refreshing breeze washes over us. Conversation stops, as we consider yet another close friend's story of heartrending loss similar to our own.

"Seems like those two phone calls, each involving a person you loved, will forever define that awful period in your life," Rick says.

"Not only that period," whispers David, barely loud enough to be heard.

"I suppose they will," Tom says. "Funny, isn't it, how certain events and people intersect and overlap somehow, coloring our recollections when we look back on them decades later?"

Grinning, remembering happy times he shared with his dad long ago, Tom appears momentarily mollified, maybe even at peace with himself. Then, abruptly, he turns somber again. "It was Dad who, through his contacts, helped arrange for the abortion. That was a loving act I will always remember him doing for me, for us, even though it broke my heart."

Over the next hour or a little more, the three of us share recollections of our parents and their suicides. As hard as this is, it's easier with close friends who lived through the same hell. They understand -- instantly and completely -- all that's being said and, perhaps more crucially, all that's being left unsaid.

Chapter VII

....

April 28-29, 2005

....

From: Rick
To: Tom
Subject: Sharing of Souls
Date: April 28, 2005

Hi Tom!

Hope all is well in NZ. An interesting challenge David has presented us.

What are you thinking about re: your trip to the U.S.? Another Labor Day swing through the Land of Cleve?

How are you and the fantastic Jen doing?

— Rick

From: **Dennis**
To: David, Tom, Rick
Subject: *Count Me In*
Date: April 29, 2005

Gents, I too will share some stuff in response to David's questions about suicide, etc.

I've been planning to write about rediscovering my mother – who killed herself in the mid-'70s – but have been putting it off. For what reason? Not sure. Will examine this and share some of it.

This may prompt me to finally write the article I've been procrastinating about, in which case I'll keep all the good turns of phrases to myself.

Initially when told of my mother's death and the circumstances, I felt guilt and embarrassment. I told precious few people how she died. I remember the day and what I was doing as clearly as I remember sitting in class and hearing about JFK.

How soon do you want this stuff, David?

More later.

Peace, Dennis

P.S. David, I can't recall how it was that we learned of this "secret" we share. Do you remember? I do recall talking about our mothers at length at a St. Louis Cards game, but we had known about the suicides for some time.

Chapter VIII

....

June, 2002

....

St. Louis, MO

· ·

A nd now, with Dennis' email, the fourth of the sons of suicide has weighed in.

Dennis' inclusion in the "fraternity" shares striking similarities with Tom's. In this case, Dennis and David had come to know each other casually when they both lived and worked in Southern California, although their professional circles barely and rarely overlapped. Dennis was a journalist and a writer and marketer for a host of clients, while David was a member of the School of Communications faculty at Cal State Fullerton. Other than quick hellos at meetings of the professional association to which they both belonged, they knew little of one another.

But that changed in the early '90s when they each moved away, Dennis to a sprawling new house in Boulder, Colorado, and David to the University of Arkansas in Fayetteville. A mutual acquaintance, a former graduate student of David's who also worked with Dennis on several projects, knew the two shared professional and avocational interests: communication, photography, writing, baseball and politics. At her prodding, they eventually connected, first with emails and soon after with occasional phone talks.

Their friend's intuition was spot on. They hit it off instantly, with conversation flowing so effortlessly that before long, their email exchanges and phone calls grew longer, deeper and more personal. Then, in yet another extraordinary twist of fate, just two weeks after David and Rick learned of Tom's father's suicide, Dennis divulged to David during a casual phone chat that his long-depressed mother killed herself with a pistol in the prime of her life, when Dennis was a young professional building his career.

It would be several years before David and Dennis would delve into the harrowing experiences of their mothers' suicides. The setting for that impromptu discussion was, of all places, a nearly empty Busch Stadium in St. Louis, home of the Cardinals baseball club.

Before then, any talk of their mothers' fates had been as faceless voices through a phone line or typed words in emails, neither of which is all that conducive to sharing private, painful, tucked away thoughts and unresolved feelings.

. . . .

"Denny, when you think back to the time right after your mom shot herself . . . what stands out most, aside from the obvious?"

Even though they are nearly alone in the eerily quiet, cavernous ballpark during batting practice, David poses the question in a voice barely above a whisper, a long-held reflex whenever suicide is mentioned.

Dennis considers the not-so-simple question but remains focused on the field, where the flurry of balls flying off bats and into gloves slows, and heads turn as Cardinals' slugger Albert Pujols, reigning rookie of the year, steps toward the batting cage.

"Hard to say really," Dennis says. "A bunch of things, I guess. Like my boss showing up at the funeral. That surprised me, pleasantly so." He grins slightly at the memory. "And my sister . . . well, she barely spoke to me then and for the longest time, so pissed off was she at me for the, uh, gruff way she thought I broke the news to her that Mom took her own life."

"Is there an un-gruff way to say that?" David smirks, rising to Denny's defense. "How'd you put it when you told her?"

He thinks about that for a time, then seems at a loss. "Damned if I can remember. Probably something crass, like 'Mom blew her head off.' I was angry. And back then, I tended to shoot my mouth off first, and think about it later." Again, Dennis smiles to himself, and likely at himself. "But what may've gotten to me more than anything was how my mother's family blamed my father, *viciously* blamed him, for, for . . . well, for *everything*. And how that splintered my family, on both sides."

"Boy, do I know about that," David mutters.

Instantly, Denny spins to face him, an incredulous expression fast-spreading across his face. "No shit. Your mother's family did the same?"

David nods, then shakes his head in disgust. "Same thing with Rick, who I've told you about. His grandmother, his mother's mother for Christ's sake, wouldn't have anything to do with him or his siblings . . . as if it were somehow *their* fault."

"Ugly stuff," Dennis murmurs gloomily, then looks away, fighting back tears.

For several minutes, they both seem content just watching batting practice, though their minds are elsewhere, somewhere in the distant past, yearning to rewrite history.

"Listening to you got me thinking about my mother's funeral," David muses, sounding a bit philosophical. "A day I've tried to forget . . . but can't." He waits until Denny looks at him. "I was allowed to attend the funeral in Brooklyn, but my sister, who was only nine, wasn't. Neither of us went to the burial afterwards in Queens. I'm pretty sure it was my first funeral, so I didn't know what to expect." As he drifts back to that terrible time and place, his eyes slowly close, as if he's able to see himself at 13 again – that confused, lost boy who was supposed to be chanting bar mitzvah prayers but instead was saying Kaddish for his dead mother.

"I'm inches from the casket, but can't bring myself to touch it . . . it was closed, made of dark wood, really big and shiny. My knees buckled when I thought of her in there, lying still as a stone. I kept asking myself, 'Is she really in there?' Somebody handed me a handkerchief that smelled of cologne, or perfume, but the tears didn't come until later. After that, I don't recall much, except my wailing grandmother hanging onto one of my arms and my sobbing aunt, my mother's sister in whose home she swallowed the sleeping pills, clinging to the other. They hated my father, dumped all their anger and blame on him . . . saving not even a little for themselves. After that, everything's just a blur."

Once they started talking, Dennis and David didn't stop – couldn't stop – until they heard the national anthem playing.

While they'll never remember which team won the game or who hit home runs, they'll always remember what happened during batting practice.

. . . .

Talking about our parents' suicides is never easy, for any of us. Indeed, few things are harder. When we do open up, about as often as a lunar eclipse, it's usually to those precious few we know we can trust to truly listen, try to understand, and not judge us or our parents too harshly.

Chapter IX

....

April 30–May 7, 2005

....

From: **David**
To: Dennis
cc: Rick, Tom
Subject: *A Little Background*
Date: April 30, 2005

Dennis, you mentioned the guilt and embarrassment we have all felt at one time or another. Does it ever go away, completely? Why is that, I wonder, even now?

And yep, Tommy is now in New Zealand for several years, having moved there with his wife Jenny after he retired as a crackerjack newsman with the Voice of America in Washington. Wait until you hear his deep, resonant voice – you'll know why he was a broadcaster and, in my view, a terrific one. He, Rick and I met early in our careers in the Washington, D.C., area.

Interestingly, however, it wasn't until many years later, while on a baseball road trip, that we happened into conversation that revealed we three – we couldn't believe it! – shared parental suicides in our histories. Not a topic that tends to pop up in everyday casual conversation, is it?

Anyway, since we seem to be locking arms on this, thought you should have a better idea how all this came to be. More will emerge naturally as we go, I'm sure.

Talk to you tomorrow, Denny . . . Shalom, David

From: **Dennis**
To: David
cc: Tom , Rick
Subject: *On the Couch*
Date: April 30, 2005

David —

Re: embarrassment. I thought perhaps that it might be unique with me – or at least the extent of my embarrassment.

I can't say for certain why I was embarrassed. Because it was like saying my mother was unbalanced, or downright loony? For some time, I felt that way but do not any more. I have few reservations about telling people how my mother died. Is it the openness of society today? Or my coming to grips with my mother's problems – which included long-term alcoholism?

Perhaps – I just thought of this – the embarrassment and guilt may stem from a fear that people will think I either contributed to the conditions – alcoholism and suicide – or at least was negligent in doing something about it. Now, that's something to think about.

I feel as if I'm on the couch.

More later.

— Dennis

From: **David**
To: Dennis
cc: Rick, Tom
Subject: *All in the Family - And As You Like It*
Date: April 30, 2005

Thanks much, Denny, for your willingness to share your thoughts and feelings in response to my nosy, emotionally charged questions.

Perhaps in doing so, you'll fuel your own motivation to write the article about your Mom you've had in mind for some time. We all need a trigger now and again to jumpstart us to do what we've wanted to do but for whatever reason just couldn't take the first step.

As far as your responses go, there's no set timetable. I know well the angst that comes with dredging up feelings and memories on this ultra-sensitive subject, but the sooner the better, from my standpoint. As I noted to Tom in an earlier email, I'll happily take all you're willing to share, in whatever form and length easiest for you. Not to worry about anything you want to say to us. Confidentiality will always be honored.[3]

When Rick and I met as 17-year-olds, we were still very much confused and lost, in need of somebody with whom we could share this "burden" of ours, as I still think of it. Somehow, though the need has diminished in the years since, it never goes away. My hope is that in sharing our fears, revelations, good and bad times, insights and observations, each of us will be helped just as Rick and I were as perplexed teenagers. Soon, we'll all be on that virtual couch, presumably comparing notes and experiences, revealing parts of our inner selves.

Please know in advance, friends, how grateful I am for whatever you're comfortable contributing to the discussion.

You spoke of feeling embarrassed, Dennis, which I fully understand. In part, the embarrassment arises, I believe, from thinking we'll be viewed as tainted, as somehow genetically weak and unbalanced (as you pointed out). Like mother or father, like son, sort of thing. For a long, long time, I think that twisted thinking held me in its grasp.

---

[3] This book, including all references and words attributed to them, is published with Tom's and Dennis' permission, approval and encouragement.

Also, I suppose I've always felt a bit embarrassed divulging this "secret" in my life, even if long ago in my past, due to the position it puts the other person in; what can they say, what should they say, though they invariably feel compelled to say something, anything, that is typically inappropriate and/or unhelpful. It's human nature, right?

And I don't want to be asked questions I don't want to answer, or can't. Attempting to field such distasteful queries invariably causes all parties to the conversation to feel awkward and rude, regardless of the words exchanged.

Anyway, let the discussions continue . . . David

From: **Rick**
To: David, Tom, Dennis
Subject: Embarrassment
Date: May 1, 2005

Hello, Dennis, Tom and David —

I guess it's my turn to join the discussion . . . though it will be a few days before I can offer a more complete response.

Interesting that you felt embarrassed, because that's not how I would have described myself at the time (or now). I did consider my mother's suicide a deeply personal and intimate issue, so it's not as if I wandered about school (I was 14) talking a lot about it. Instead, I'd characterize my reaction as one of devastation.

My father, on the other hand, was clearly embarrassed. He called the editor of the *Dayton Daily News*, an Air Force Reserve buddy, and asked that any article regarding her death not indicate it was a suicide. The editor was kind enough to comply.

Dad didn't tell us that Mom had intentionally killed herself. Somewhere along the way, I learned she had left a note. I never saw it, but I understand it said simply, "Mark, now there are no more problems." My brother didn't see it either, but was told the note read, "Mark, your position is no longer untenable" – a subtle but significant difference. We each vividly remember the precise words.

However the note was worded, it raises questions I just can't answer: What were the problems? What was untenable? What was so problematic, so untenable that Mom felt her only solution was to end her life? In our family, the adults didn't argue in front of the children. My parents addressed issues behind closed doors. So I have no clue what the underlying meaning of the note was, and I can only speculate. Did it have to do with family finances? With Dad's job? With the loneliness I assume Mom felt being so far from her family? Might there have been a third person involved?

Dad went so far as to say that Mom's jottings probably weren't really a suicide note because she always signed or initialed her notes. It likely was the start of a longer, thoughtful list of actions the two of them could take to address some unspecified issues, he said. If she had finished what she was writing, she would

haunt me: If Dad could have just made it through that rock bottom day, was another attempt on his life just a matter of time? Or if he got beyond that day, might he and his family and counseling, etc., have lifted that terrible burden he carried?

So who's to blame . . . mere mortals or the Heavenly Father who my minister tells me has a reason for all He does?

Down to Cases

Sorry guys, it's a bit after midnight on the east coast and I may be getting a bit punchy after a couple of long days. I'll never know for sure what drove my Dad over the edge. I gradually emerged from deep grief and was greeted by a terrible loneliness. I'd lost my father and my best friend in the world. How could he do this to me, my sister and my loving mother who had bent over backwards to be there for Dad, to help him every way she knew how, keeping a close eye on the two of us children while holding down a full-time job as a high school history teacher?

Dad was damaged goods, or had become so over the years. Like his father, he enjoyed liquor. Unlike his father, he eventually became an alcoholic. He worked long days and the grain and grind finally got to him. While driving home one night after one too many drinks, his car strayed across the center line of a busy highway and collided with another auto, killing the driver. Dad escaped with a few cuts and bruises, but the incident left him scarred for life.

A Deteriorating Dad

Through the years, he suffered several nervous breakdowns and was in and out of mental hospitals.

It breaks my heart when I think about how this hurt my Mom, so loving and giving to all she met, and my sister. A father and son often share a special bond and that was the case with Dad and me. I look at photos from earlier days, when he and Mom were courting and after they were married. He was so handsome and they seemed so happy . . . they were for most of a lifetime, certainly when my sister and I were born and during the good, then increasingly difficult, years.

Dad worked at the bank for a while, then at Dailey Motors in Albion (NY). He was such a natural at selling cars. Sometimes I went to the showroom and watched this "people person" work his magic. I'm blessed to have inherited many fine qualities from my parents, but a natural ease with people I owe most of all to Dad.

I'm jumping around too much, guys, between chunks of narrative and stuff more useful to Davey. Let me conclude this "bite size" morsel with a few personal observations. For most of my three years with the Army, I was stationed at Tripler Army Medical Center in Honolulu, providing varied audio-visual support for doctors' briefings and special meetings as well as assisting the Commanding General by reading aloud messages of praise for soldiers receiving a variety of medals for acts of bravery and heroism. All had been treated for their wounds at Tripler and were recuperating there.

As the Vietnam conflict raged far away, a call from home brought word of Dad's death. It wasn't until after I returned that Mom and I had the conversation that shed light on a situation I knew from afar was deteriorating. There were times when Dad would be away from home for weeks at a time. He'd come home but couldn't remember where he'd been or why he went. I never imagined how soon Dad would feel this was the only way he could say good-bye . . . to us and to his life.

I was devastated. I'd lost my Dad and best friend . . . a person who had always been there for me. How could he throw away all the good times and great memories we and our family shared? I felt angry and confused, but the more I tried to lash out the more depressed I became. I was ashamed and terribly disillusioned that Dad chose to end his life without somehow acknowledging those of us who had been the loves of his life, especially for all that Mom endured during those dreadful last years. I was embarrassed and mad that, in deference to many people's comfort levels and small town expectations of respected members of the community, we often tip-toed around the "s" word.

Keep the faith, guys, I'm almost out of gas!

I continue to agonize over the fact that I wasn't there when Dad and Mom needed me most. If I had been there, would it have made a difference – or just postponed the inevitable? I'm trying to understand what Dad was feeling and why things had gotten to the point where he believed the best thing for him to do was "go quietly into the good night." Did his alcoholism, mental illness, emphysema from smoking more than two packs of Camels a day – and the sense of inadequacy he felt when compared to Mom – cumulatively outweigh the deep and abiding love of his family? The answer, sadly, is yes. And I've spent lots of time beating myself up over the years about why I couldn't find a connection with him that would've pulled him back from the brink.

On that note, I'll close for now.

All the best, Tommy

From: **David**
To: Tommy
cc: Rick, Dennis
Subject: The Questions Persist
Date: May 2, 2005

Tommy, I'm grateful to you for sharing so openly and candidly the first installment of your story. Your deep-seated emotions seep through in every sentence: the pain, the confusion, the guilt, the regret, the frustration, the wanting, the wishing to find plausible answers to impossible questions – all of it.

You spoke of much I didn't know about your Dad, and you, and the circumstances that led him to choose suicide. I'm eager to hear more. Especially what happened after his death, soon after and in the years that followed. How did his death by his own hand change you? Influence how you've lived your life? And how have your memories of him shifted, if at all, as you've moved farther away from the day of that terrible phone call?

I imagine I speak for Dickie and Dennis when I say how instantly and thoroughly I related to your mixed feelings after your Dad's death – particularly the haunting questions you posed. Oh, the questions, the what ifs, the if onlys. They never go away, do they, no matter how many times and different ways we attempt to unravel them. Seeking answers that don't exist. And won't ever, since they died with the only ones truly capable of explaining why our parents were incapable of figuring out how to fix what was broken inside them.

We seem to hold onto the false hope that somehow our pain will be eased and our confusion clarified if we can find tolerable answers to intolerable questions.

I often wonder if these nagging, insoluble queries comprise the most enduring legacy a parent who chooses suicide leaves to a child. The questions are forever; they persist and persist, one moment looming larger, the next fading smaller, but always lingering nearby, unsettled and ever ominous.

With the warmest of thoughts of you, of Jenny, of Annie, of us four, I wish you well. . . . Davey

From: **Tommy**
To: Davey
cc: Rick, Dennis
Subject: *Writing and Remembering*
Date: May 4, 2005

Thanks for the feedback, Davey.

Writing about Dad was surprising in a way . . . I haven't spent that much time in many months writing intensely for two straight days (at least 12 hours, including painful recollections). The emotions when I think about him are still soft to the touch, after nearly 38 years – and the effort of mining my feelings and then trying to express them so you and others might comprehend what I find so hard to put into words left me exhausted, yet strangely uplifted (and unburdened?).

The weight of my burden – *what I might have done* – will never dissipate, but right now it doesn't feel as heavy as before my writing about it and remembering what it felt like.

After I catch my breath in a couple of days, I'll address some of the other points you raised about how this life-altering event has (re)shaped my life and how I've lived it since Dad made his fateful decision.

Give my love to Karen and lots to you, dear friend!

Until next time,

Tommy

From: Rick
To: Tom
cc: David, Dennis
Subject: "What I Might've Done"
Date: May 5, 2005

Trying to answer the question of why our parents took their own lives is, I imagine, as complicated as any involving the human psyche.

The question is fraught with varying and conflicting perspectives and interpretations. Each of our home and family situations was different, as were – and are – our reactions to our parents' self-inflicted deaths. All four of us have tried to make rational sense of a seemingly irrational act. Our parents ended their lives to escape their unendurable pain. And perhaps they also wanted to spare those close to them – including us – unhappiness they believed they were inflicting on us. The paradox is that by taking their own lives, they heaped inconceivable agony on us.

Tom, you spoke of the "burden" you've carried since your father's suicide – the burden of what you wished you'd done but didn't. Or couldn't. I picked up on that term – burden – because, coincidentally, David's also referred to the "burden" he's carried, and believes all four of us do, by virtue of his inability to reconcile his mother's repeated attempts at suicide before she finally succeeded only days after he reached 13.

I certainly recognize that my mother's suicide is forever a part of me, has helped shape who I am. But I'm not sure I feel as you both do about her suicide being a burden. I'm curious to hear more from you about why you do and how it's affected you, negatively and positively. And, to the extent you have blamed yourself, have you been able to find a way to forgive yourself?

Interesting, isn't it, how each time one of us opens up, shares what he so rarely shares, it sparks a range of reactions, recollections, emotions, and insights from the other three of us descendants of suicide parents – as the process takes us deeper within ourselves and closer to one another . . .

Starting to wonder if we've created among ourselves a therapy group that's long overdue?

— Rick

From: **Tom**
To: Rick
cc: David, Dennis
Subject: *Could I Have Made THE Difference*
Date: May 6, 2005

Rickster, you gently prodded me to more fully explain the origins of the burden I've always felt because I wasn't there, physically and otherwise, for my Dad when he became unable to cope with his own guilt and inadequacies, and began entertaining dark and dreary urges to end his life as a way to unburden the lives of those closest to him. Namely, Mom, my sister, and me.

How could he think that? Why wasn't I there to help him see himself and the situation differently? I'll try in a few words to describe my feelings and why I feel as I do.

I can't pretend to know the answers to the many questions that still tug at my conscience, but when all was said and done, I believe Dad added up the pluses and minuses of his life and, family notwithstanding, made the most lonely and awful decision a human being can make. It was a misguided decision that left our family in a state of unspeakable grief. It was impossible then, with me heading back to Hawaii in a few days for more military service, to move beyond the funeral service and the all-consuming paralysis that followed.

Initially, I mostly felt a seething anger toward Dad for his foolish, thoughtless act of killing himself so he could escape his misery – and in so doing, bringing misery to those of us who loved him unconditionally. He terminated our very special father-son relationship, a loss beyond words. As

the eldest among us, I'm amazed now to look back and realize that my initial rage has wilted over the years, as I've gradually become more thoughtful, more forgiving, I suppose. I still feel deep pain when I consider his fractured state of mind when he slashed his wrists, but I can't stop struggling to somehow try to make sense of things. Even today, I catch myself thinking about the emotional baggage he must've carried when it all became too much for him to live with himself and the family he could no longer face.

Ultimately, I've accepted the sad truth that his unyielding disappointment in himself – as a person, as a husband, as a father – led to his suicide.

Yet, despite that belief, I've relentlessly wrestled with the pointed question, the self-accusation, over the years and finally, only recently, I came to the conclusion that the terrible truth is no. My father's suicide, sadly, was a tragedy waiting to happen at a time when he felt life was no longer worth living and the only thing that mattered to him was reaching that last awful day. For my part, it's not a case of me seeking a rationale for the guilt I felt for so long, but rather acceptance of a callous, distasteful reality I'd rather not acknowledge.

I so wish I knew the particulars of what ultimately brought him to the point of no return, willing to abandon the struggle and me, but I know I never will. Yet, the wanting never stops.

· · · · · · · · · · · · · · · · ·

But what about me and my obligation to Dad?

What else could I have done – even being far from home during my four years of undergraduate study in Ohio and then my military service in Hawaii – to make a greater difference in my father's life that might've swayed him from his fateful decision? I've spent more than a few sleepless nights grappling with that most telling of questions, filled with second thoughts of what might have been. His life of heavy drinking and smoking, the deadly accident he caused that claimed the life of another motorist that eventually landed him in a mental hospital – all these things contributed to my father's unhappiness, depression and growing lack of self-esteem. I know that. Still, though, the irksome question won't cease: Did the fact that I wasn't around, a sad reality for both of us, add to pushing my father over the edge? As the only son of an only son, I wasn't required to sign up with the U.S. Army; I enlisted by choice. But when I got that call regarding Dad's death in 1967 it was as if he was making a final plea for me to come home. The man who I deeply loved and had done so much for me throughout my life did not have me around when he might have needed me the most.

Within a few days after his funeral, I was back in sun-drenched Hawaii, going through degrees of my own depression and endless second-guessing, slipping closer and closer to where I think my father lost the battle with himself. Selfishly, looking back on that troubling time, if I hadn't returned I would never have gone on the blind date that brought me Jenny, the love of my life, more than 45 years ago.

· · · · · · · · · · · · · · · · ·

But it was that blind date that brought the brightest and most hopeful light into my life, just when I needed it. My barracks roommate, his girlfriend, Jenny and I piled into my Triumph convertible and drank in the majestic scenery of the Pali mountain range while swimming freely in the refreshing waters below. Needless to say, it was most therapeutic and in the words of Nat King Cole's infectiously beautiful love song, *That Sunday, That Summer*. "If I had to choose but one day to spend my life with you!"

She was a source of continual happiness that has only grown more intense since our marriage in Hawaii on December 23, 1970, vows we still honor today.

Which is not to say I suddenly forgot about Dad and all the memories we shared for so many wonderful years. The love we felt for one another was too deep to be shrugged off, and I continued questioning if things might have turned out differently had I been closer to Dad when he needed me most. But what Jenny brought me was a sense of perspective that pulled me from drowning in my sorrow. Suddenly, she became my true reason for living.

And so, Rick, I've come to an uneasy understanding with myself about Dad's tragic end. I've stopped feeling guilty, or as guilty, about my absence when he was at his worst; I was where I was supposed to be, doing the things I was supposed to be doing. Yet, if I'm truly honest with myself, I'll never stop wondering, "What if I'd been there?"

Oh, those pesky questions. Always the questions.

Love to all three of you and your lovely spouses,

— Tommy

Indeed, Tommy, I know well what you mean about the act of dredging up old emotions and memories being simultaneously soothing and depressing – as well as exhausting.

Maybe it's the mere act of letting go of pent-up thoughts and feelings deep inside us, always chiseling away at our souls and psyches, always crouched in the bushes ready to pounce at the slightest provocation, that can give us temporary relief from the irksome questions that never cease begging for answers that don't exist.

Is our fate, our burden, then, to forever seek unsettling, unsatisfactory answers to nightmarish questions? Or is our salvation to be found in the constant search for better answers?

· · · · · · · · · · · · · · · ·

To what extent are we our parents' keepers? Where does our obligation to them, and to ourselves, begin and end? Do we ever truly know our parents other than as parents? How far are we, the children, the sons, expected to go to please and accommodate our down-in-the-dumps parents before we've gone too far?

I know what you're thinking, Tommy. More questions. Indeed, they go on.

Your last, poignantly written email focused on the overpowering guilt you carried with you for decades after your Dad's suicide. You drew me into your irreconcilable dilemma between trying to be the good son who somehow should've saved his father from self-destruction and trying to stay true to your own desires and destiny, wherever it took you.

Though I was considerably younger than you when my mother swallowed a lethal amount of sedatives – barely 13 – I, too, wondered for many years how I may've contributed, unknowingly or otherwise, to her brutal unhappiness. Like you, and I'm sure Rick and Dennis too, questioning my role, or lack of, in the baffling circumstances surrounding my mother's suicide leads only to a dead end. A dead end that holds no definitive answers to the disconcerting questions we can't seem to stop asking.

At the time of my mother's death, as questions and blame flew like poison darts in every direction, I hadn't yet connected the scattered dots encompassing her, my father's and my extended families' past. But I needed to, more than anything; and even more than knowing what had happened, I needed to know *why* things happened as they did. But the adults in my life either couldn't, or wouldn't, give me anything more than vague, mushy explanations or their skewed, finger-pointing version of the so-called truth.

That is, except my uncle Ben . . . who, to me and those close to me, was always Unc. Just Unc.

· · · · · · · · · · · · · · · · ·

In the days leading up to my mother's funeral and burial, I never left Unc's side.

I shadowed him everywhere, and he didn't seem to mind. If he got in the car to do an errand, I was in the shotgun seat. If he stepped out for a walk, I was alongside him. All the while, we talked, I mean really talked. Man to man, not man to boy. And no topic was taboo.

I pelted him with a tirade of questions and hypotheses, pressing him to tell me things, some ugly and sensitive about my parents – things no adult had been willing to share with me, a wet-behind-the-ears kid who'd barely entered his teen years. Questions about my mother, my father, their marriage, my mother's early life and prior suicide attempts, my mother's mother and sister (both of whom blamed my father for everything, including her death), events I'd witnessed but hadn't understood sufficiently to connect the dots, and what was likely and unlikely to happen next. And, of course, with every query I wanted to know *why*, or why *not*.

And Unc never flinched. Never dodged a question, no matter how disquieting its revelations or implications. Never gave me a wishy-washy, sugar-coated, or watered down explanation. He was blunt and unstintingly honest, no holds barred almost to a fault (as some, like my aunt, believed), never shied away from adding his interpretation or opinion, and when he didn't think he knew enough to take a stand one way or the other, he said so.

He treated me as an adult who could think and process information intelligently, not a kid who needed shielding from his own life, however tragic and bizarre. In truth, I'd been forced to grow up years before, for my own and my sister's sake, to offset my mother's inability to cope with her own problems and my father's innate inadequacies as a husband and father.

Unc seemed to intuitively understand that if I was going to find my way through this deteriorating predicament that was likely to get worse before it got better, I was going to have to figure things out, to the extent possible, for myself. To my satisfaction. Nobody else's. What others (including him) believed I should, or shouldn't, know – or believe – didn't matter.

And so, encouraged by my uncle's invaluable gift of helping me to seek my own truth, that's what I've been doing ever since. If I hadn't, I'm not sure if much would've ever made sense to me. Or how differently I might've turned out or lived my life. I know I'll never know all I want to know. But, thanks to Unc being Unc, I know far more than I would have otherwise.

Thank you, Tommy, for triggering this wistful memory of a time when one man's unrelenting honesty kept a young man's world from crumbling.

Take a breather before continuing with your story; you've earned it. But know this as you do: We three really do get what you're saying, and feeling, and that you are giving to us – and hopefully to you too – something invaluable, unavailable anywhere else.

Be well, my good friend . . . Davey

Chapter X

....

June, 2002

....

Bowie, MD

. . . .

With suicides, news of a loved one's death almost always comes as a shock so staggering it spawns instant denial – and innumerable *why* questions that will never stop begging for answers. With natural death, whether sudden or drawn out over months or years, comes inevitable sadness, the pain of loss, and, if it ends unendurable suffering, a contradictory sense of relief.

Yet one paradox of death, whatever the cause, is that it brings people together. And, quite often, prompts the sharing of memories too long forgotten, and the resolving of issues too unnerving to face.

Death is, after all, much more about the living than the dead.

. . . .

David's Uncle Ben passed away quietly during the night, his wife Phyllis' hand resting gently on his chest.

A few weeks earlier, David talked with him at his bedside, heart to heart, suspecting – knowing, actually – it was the last time. "Though I didn't call him Dad," David tells Rick from Chicago's O'Hare between flights after that final visit with his failing uncle, "and he didn't refer to me as his son, we both knew . . ." – his voice cracks, forcing a pause – ". . . what we meant to each other."

"Anybody who knows you well or has spent time with the two of you knows it, too," Rick empathizes, as only he can. Ben and Phyllis always embraced him as not only David's friend but as another nephew, feelings he reciprocated – regardless of the passage of time between visits.

Within hours of receiving word of his uncle's death, David is on his way to Bowie from his home in Arkansas. He arrives as the last of the local condolence-wishers are hugging Phyllis on the front porch of the modest two-story house on Kayhill Lane, the safe haven offered to him for his final year of high school when his life was adrift and he thought he was out of options, and where he and Rick first disclosed their dark secret to each other. But on this day, the home he remembers as filled with warmth and unconditional acceptance seems unfamiliar, strangely unrecognizable, and, most upsetting, absent Ben's indelible presence.

Despite the late hour, David, Phyllis and her daughters share a few tears, along with bittersweet smiles, recalling Ben's dry-as-dust sense of humor and volatile mood swings, swapping anecdotes of his best, worst and zaniest moments.

"He had the biggest mouth and the biggest heart . . ." David says, seized by a pang of melancholy, and the stone cold realization that his stand-in father is now part of his past, ". . . and he never shut either of them."

"Ain't that the truth," Phyllis concurs, smiling and weeping at the same time.

. . . .

The following day, shortly before noon, an unexpected knock on the front door echoes through the quiet house.

David rises slowly from his uncle's favorite chair on the backyard screened-in patio, wanting to spare his aunt "greeting" duty. For the past hour, he's been out there alone with his memories. But a jumpy Phyllis, who fielded one phone call after another all morning, is a couple steps in front of him and, without checking the peephole, pulls open the door.

"Oh my," she yelps softly, hands flying to her cheeks. She does a double-take at the visitor standing at her doorstep. "I can't believe it . . . come in, come in."

Rick steps into the foyer, hands hidden behind his back, and flashes a mischievous grin that transports Phyllis back in time. Then, in one swift move, he holds up a jumbo-size package of Oreo cookies in one hand and a plastic half-gallon of milk in the other. The combo was our #1 after-school snack in high school, frequently served up by Phyllis, who savored those sweet little sandwiches as much as we did.

"You remembered," she gushes, bloodshot eyes filling with a new batch of tears, and hugs Rick hard and long.

Approaching the foyer, David looks up – and halts in his tracks.

All he can do is stare in silence, jaw slightly agape, at the implausible sight of his friend of some 35 years. Then, with the faintest of smiles, David points to the commemorative snack food Rick is holding up proudly, as if it were an Olympic gold medal. "He never forgets the good stuff, Aunt. Do you, Dickie?"

"Why would I?" Rick counters, grabbing David in a tight bear hug. Then, stepping back from the friend he came to console, he adds, "The good stuff's the best stuff."

Nodding, David falters back half a step as his knees go weak, momentarily overcome by the mingling of clashing emotions bubbling up inside him. Still overcome by the sight of Rick appearing out of the blue, he murmurs, "Are you a ghost, a dream, or what?" He blinks rapidly, expectantly, as if trying to peer through fog – or back in time. "Where, uh, did you come from and, uh, and how did you get here?"

Rick clearly relishes watching David sputtering like a faulty engine. "Well, let's see. Came from Cleveland, where I live? . . . and got here the usual way, car, plane, car, you know the routine."

"Okay, okay," David holds up both hands, having been chastised enough for his feeble language. "Dumb question. So, let me put it another way – "

Rick jumps in, not done yet. "Though finding this place wasn't as easy as I remember. But I got here – with only one wrong turn."

"Reallllly?" David's voice rises in challenge. "What's it been, 25, 30 years since you drove these streets?"

"Okay . . . two wrong turns," Rick comes back, a little too fast.

The game is on. "You sure about that?"

Winking, Rick admits nothing. Then, as if suddenly tapped on the shoulder, he takes notice of the now-worn, yet still comfy house he remembers vividly and fondly where he was always welcome – and always had a place at the kitchen table.

"I got here, didn't I?"

"Indeed you did, indeed you did. Miracles never cease."

We share furtive grins, our way of acknowledging to one another that "it's us, back together again" – and so ridiculing, razzing, harassing and the like are fair game.

But David's playful demeanor quickly evaporates for no apparent reason. Except there is a reason: he needs to know why Rick came when it was understood, at least by David, that he wouldn't. "But tell me, no kidding," he says pointedly, head tilted in waiting, "what compelled you to come? I told you weeks ago it wasn't necessary. That you shouldn't feel obligated. I'd understand."

Rick is flustered by David's puzzling insistence that he answer a question David should already know the answer to. But, Rick tells himself, this isn't a day for tiffs or overreactions or bruised feelings, so he lets it pass as if unnoticed. "I didn't feel an obligation to come . . . just a strong desire." Then, after allowing his words to sink in, Rick's eyes brighten to a twinkle and he adds with exactly the right pinch of exaggeration, "Besides, I figured you'd need a proper snack right about now."

David eyes the oversized package of Oreos, and can't hold back an "I give up" shrug of the shoulders. "Did you now . . . *really?*"

"Lunch in fifteen, boys," Phyllis announces in a case of perfect timing, turning and heading for the kitchen. Then, as if we were still scruffy teenagers, "Don't forget to wash up . . . with soap, please!"

Some things never change, no matter how old we get. Thank goodness.

. . . .

After a light lunch topped off with Oreos dipped in milk, we decide to take a "flashback" tour of Bowie before Rick has to return to BWI for his flight home.

For a time, we drive around aimlessly, catching glimpses of familiar landmarks from our high school days and making easy conversation catching up on mutual friends and family members.

First stop on the nostalgia tour is Rick's old house at the far end of the Lerner Place cul-de-sac. It holds enduring memories from the early days of a burgeoning friendship, yet appears unchanged by time. Next we drive to where it began for us: the school bus stop where Rick was lost and David "rescued" him just in the nick of time (that interpretation, according to David).

Finally, we return to the bench in Fox Hill Park, where we talked for hours, took the measure of each other, predicted pennant races, foretold our futures – and revealed, with a frankness that surprised even us at that time, our doubts and disappointments, as well as our hopes and still-emerging dreams.

· · · · · · · · · · · · · · · ·

"Your coming today . . . it means a lot, y'know," says David, voice trembling slightly, peering intently at Rick from the passenger seat of the roomy rental car, now parked on the driveway of the Kayhill Lane house. "To Aunt. To me. To Unc, who, if he were here" – his eyes close, and he points to the heavens – "would tell you the same thing Aunt told you earlier today: You're a *mensch*, Richard J. Knapp. And coming from him, there's no higher compliment. As we both know, he was always pretty stingy with the compliments."

David clears his throat several times, stalling. "You really didn't have to do this. There's no funeral or memorial service, nothing formal. Unc's wishes. So why did you?"

Rick looks at him askance. "Why wouldn't I?"

"I can think of reasons . . ."

"Reasons?" Rick is genuinely clueless. "What reasons?" David shrugs, which only puzzles Rick further. "I couldn't think of anything appropriate to scribble in a sappy Hallmark card. So I started thinking about Ben, about you, about Aunt Phyllis, and, well . . . here I am."

When no response comes, Rick looks expectantly over at David, met only by the back of his friend's head peering intently out the passenger side window. He waits for David to turn around, to say something, anything, but he seems stuck in place, his mind far, far away.

"What's bothering you, JD?"

David stirs uncomfortably but can't bring himself to say what's on his mind. "Not sure this is the right time for it," he finally mutters, as if more for himself than Rick.

"Right time for *what*?" Rick fires back, unable to hide his surging frustration.

"Okay, okay, okay," David squawks testily, pinching the bridge of his nose. He opens his mouth, but nothing comes out, and he does the same thing again.

Sensing David's inner struggle, Rick leans closer to his heartbroken friend and in a calm, soft voice says, "Come on, it's me. Let it out. What's going on with you?"

David slowly twists around to confront his closest friend, as well as himself. For almost three years, he's been quietly tormented by something he didn't do and should've, something he knows he can't put off acknowledging any longer. But he hesitates anyway, allowing a few beats to pass before speaking, with eyes closed. "Wish I'd done three years ago what you did today," he says, immediately turning back to the window. "But I, I . . ."

David stops himself, weighing again whether to keep going or shut up. But then, in the blink of an eye, he realizes *this* moment won't come again. A moment, he also recognizes through the haze of his doubts he's actually been waiting for, been wanting, for what feels like an eternity.

"Your dad's memorial service. I should've been there, I . . ."

Click. Rick gets it now; it's vintage David, for better or worse. "No need to explain or apologize," he cuts off David, wanting to spare him any further agony of dumping guilt on himself unnecessarily. "We talked daily around that time, about everything. Conversations I couldn't have had with anybody else." A heartbeat later, he adds in a lighter, softer timbre, "Don't underestimate how much you helped me."

Still staring dolefully out the window, David appears not to hear a word Rick has said, but things aren't always what they seem. "When we talked the night of the memorial service you told me that one of your Cleveland friends showed up unannounced, and how much that meant to you." Pausing, he slowly turns back around and meets Rick's understanding eyes. "Don't get me wrong. I was comforted knowing you had a good friend there . . . but I felt terrible, too."

Rick flinches. "Why would you feel terrible?"

David draws in a long, labored breath. "Because . . ." – his jaw clenches tight – "it's what I thought about doing, but . . . didn't. I should've been a *mensch* . . . like you." Sighing, he shifts back to the side window again. "I'll always regret I wasn't."

"Let it go, JD," Rick says gently but resolutely, "just let it go. Our friendship is so much more than keeping score on who does what when, or doesn't. Aren't we beyond that by now?" He waits for David to turn and give him a faint nod. "We do what we can at the time, and don't sit in judgment when we can't be perfect."

Again, silence fills the car as Rick waits for David to look at him; he wants him to see that he means what he's about to say. "Look at me, please," Rick says gently, but with just the right amount of insistence. When David turns, he's blinking away tears, as Rick gazes unblinking at him. "We've *always* been there for each other, one way or another, when it's mattered most. Remember *that*, okay?"

The tension gripping David's facial features, from his creased forehead to his clenched chin, gradually slackens, turning his mien pensive, relieved. He nestles into the soft leather of the contoured bucket seat as he considers the caring, familiar face pleading with him to forgive himself.

"I will, I will. As I will *always* remember this day and . . ." – a glint moistens his eyes – ". . . the Oreos and milk."

Chapter XI

....

May 8, 2005

....

From: Dennis
To: Tom, Rick, David
Subject: To Live and Die in LA
Date: May 8, 2005

Guys —

I've only just now read Tom's powerful recounting of his father's descent into suicide. While it's weighing on my mind, I'll dive into my own past, for the benefit of David's storyline – and perhaps our own collective psyches?

Ashamed, angry, confused are words Tom used to describe his reactions and I'd second all of those emotions and more. I was at home on a Saturday morning preparing to go to work. The trade association where I worked was holding a mini retreat/seminar for its 100 or so employees. Saturday was the last day. A friend of my folks called to tell me. I don't remember if she said "killed herself" or used a euphemism, but it was something like, "Your mother killed herself, honey." I remember going back to work that Monday or Tuesday feeling embarrassed and unable to tell anyone how my mother died.

At the time of my mother's death, my (previous) wife and I were living in Southern California, about 35 miles from my folks. This was in the early '70s. We drove over there and I remember crying for about two hours. After that I was sort of in a daze. I remember calling my sister immediately, my only sibling, and telling her what had happened. She was angry with me for a long time because I didn't break it to her gently. At the time of my mother's death and for a week or two after, my mind was a psychological stew, flavored with a variety of emotions.

Background: My mother was troubled, and I'm not sure when it started. By the time I was in high school in Petaluma, she drank heavily from the afternoon on. As a stay-at-home mom, she was free to sit around and drink lots and often. Tom knows what I mean. She saw a shrink off and on, but disdained the thought she needed help. She was overly protective of me and my sister and sometimes alternated between being loving and being abusive – as her mind was distorted by booze.

In the year before she died, my mother would often call me in the evening to complain about life in general. She was lonely, resented it when my father traveled for business, and didn't have many outlets or interests other than reading and drinking. She was afraid to drive more than a few miles from our house so her world began to shrink. When my sister and I were no longer living at home, my mother lost her purpose and didn't find another. As I said, she'd call to talk and I'd urge her to get involved with clubs, organizations, community groups – anything to help her make friends and get out of the house. She'd agree with me, but then call back a day or so later saying that she couldn't do anything.

When she killed herself, I immediately thought that I had not done enough to help her. I'd been married only a few years, was trying hard to build a career, wasn't making a lot of money, and was therefore absorbed in my own life. Like Tom, I wonder if things would have turned out differently if this or if that had happened. What would have happened if she had not found one of the guns my folks kept
at home?

My mother worked on the school paper in high school, acted and wrote dramas in college. She also had talent as an artist and occasionally she'd show us kids one of the beautiful sketches she'd made in college. She talked about exploring artistic outlets, but never did anything more than talk. She left behind a life of undeveloped talents and unfulfilled promise.

I was angry that she left me, angry that she didn't give me another chance to help her. My mother's family – her sister and brothers and parents – blamed my father for my mother's death – and for the conditions that led to her suicide. My father lived for about 20 more years, but my mother's family never communicated with him. That created one of the greatest challenges of my life. I wanted to support my father, but didn't want to cut myself off from the aunts, uncles, cousins and grandparents I'd grown up with. It was a fucking mess for several years; eventually, I made my peace with my mother's family and consider them close to me today.

Other effects: I know that I am prone to drink more than I should and have thought about suicide – more than just randomly – on several occasions. Suicide (and attendant depression) is there in the back of my head, but my mother's example will assure that I keep it under control.

That's my story.

— Dennis

From: Tom
To: Dennis
cc: Rick, David
Subject: To Live and Die in LA
Date: May 8, 2005

Thank you, Dennis, for sharing that painful, difficult story of your mother's suicide. It was touching and sad, because of the unfulfilled promise you mentioned . . . all the things she could have done with her life. It's that awful sense of helplessness after the fact and the forever nagging question: on that terrible day, could I have somehow broken through and made a difference? Or like all the "empty words" about exploring artistic outlets, would your talented and creative mother, like my Dad, have killed herself some other day?

As I've mentioned, I think the short answer is yes. How much and for how long can a person endure his or her burden before reaching the point of no return? In a muddled world of confused thoughts, even the otherwise normal souls among us reach a point where the perceived negatives in life outweigh the positives. Then, I think, it's just a matter of time.

In addition to our exchange of emails, Dennis, I've been working on another segment Davey wanted me to explore: a more personalized look at how I've gotten on with my life since Dad committed suicide. I'll try to get that in the pipeline in a couple of days. Like you, the thought of suicide has crossed my mind on several occasions during periods of prolonged depression.

There have been times when I drank too much. And now, after so many years, I'm full of grand ideas and lots of talk about how I'm going to jump-start my very different life into high gear . . . followed by a deafening silence, save for the gentle purr of promises, promises! More soon.

Be well mates, Tom

Chapter XII

....

August, 2009

....

McCormick & Schmick's, Chicago, IL

· ·

As the oversized – and now empty – dinner dishes are removed by an efficient wait staff, each of us leans back into the soft leather banquettes. We are satiated with a little too much delicious food and tongue-loosening drink.

But the sweetest satisfaction, by far, is the inner sense of triumph we all feel just being together, at last . . . four scattered souls gathered around the same dinner table. Four years after pouring out our hearts and tragic stories to each other in a blunt, revealing exchange of emails.

Face-to-face-to-face-to-face for the first – and perhaps only – time.

· · · · · · · · · · · · · · · · · ·

Though the passage of time is supposed to heal all wounds, it hasn't for any of us.

The wounds cut too deep and too close to the heart to ever fully heal. Time does dull the aching, making it less constant. Sometimes, we may forget about the suicide for a time, or trick ourselves into imagining that it occurred in another life. Yet, no matter what else we do, the hurt of such an unspeakable loss is always part of us.

For each of us, as it must also be for others fated to endure a loved one's suicide, the legacy bequeathed to us is to endlessly ponder the tormenting question of *why* – that yearning to unearth the reasons that drove our parents to take the most desperate and irrevocable of human acts. "Why?" was the question we grappled with when suicide first entered our lives, and it's the very same question we ask ourselves today, decades later. If any explanation ever existed, it died with our parents, who somehow justified their final decision in life by devaluing their own lives and miscalculating – or perhaps never considering – how killing themselves would forever reshape and burden their children's lives.

As we wait for dessert menus to arrive, our recollections meander back to those murky days after our parents' suicides. Our collective mood veers toward the bittersweet. More bitter than sweet, at first.

David senses an opening to rekindle the conversation. "Guys, we've been dancing around various versions of this sticky question for years. No time like the present, as the saying goes." Three sets of curious eyes settle on him. "How much are we a reflection of the parent we lost to suicide?" he begins, struggling as his emotions begin bubbling up. "Were we, were our lives from that point on, changed by the suicide? If so, how so? Do we look back on the arc of our lives now as divided between before the suicide and after the suicide?"

At once, Dennis, Tom and Rick flash disapproving scowls at David for raising such weighty questions just as they are warming to the notion of sweets and lighter fare. None of us is eager to tackle questions that have ruthlessly unnerved us most of our lives.

Tom and Dennis study their hands. David and Rick sit motionless, staring in opposite directions.

Saving us, momentarily, is our young waiter, who seemingly materializes out of nowhere, small wooden dessert menus tucked under one arm and a yellow index card with scribbled specials in his other hand. He passes a menu to each of us, takes a step back, flashes an obligatory smile of perfectly straight, shiny white teeth, and launches into his spiel. "Gentlemen, we have three delectable dessert specials tonight. May I tell you about them? The first one is . . ."

Rick cuts him off. "Paul, we're eager to hear about those desserts, I assure you," he says civilly but firmly, winking at Tom, who already is licking his lips in anticipation, "but we're taking things slow and easy this evening, so why don't you give us a few more minutes. That okay?"

"Certainly, sir," Paul nods, not missing a beat to please. Then, after a graceful half-bow, he backpedals and vanishes as magically as he appeared.

"Smoothly done, Mr. Knapp," Dennis nods, raising his near-empty water glass in toast. Tom and David do the same. Rick says nothing, as hints of a grin play at the corners of his mouth. All eyes are on him now; he grabbed the floor, and so it is his until he relinquishes it.

After a few beats of silence, Rick leans in, angling his elbows on the edge of the table, fingers clasped tight into a knuckled ball. "When my mother died," he says wistfully, voice barely perceptible, "she was just shy of her 40th birthday. She'd be in her mid-80s today. That's hard for me to picture. Even harder to believe, though, is that I've lived half again as long as she did."

Stopping to absorb his own words, Rick shakes his head at this disconcerting comparison of his mother's abbreviated life to his own.

"Thinking about her that way makes me wonder . . ." His voice tapers off, giving way to a swell of emotions. ". . . Uh, wonder about so many things. Like what would she have been like in her 60s and 70s if she had spit out those pills instead of swallowing them?"

A faraway gaze rolls up in Rick's dark eyes. Perhaps he is picturing his mother as he imagines she would look today.

Then his pace quickens as the questions surge. "How would her presence in my life during all those years she was absent have changed who I became? Would her unhappiness, her depression, have dragged me down, too? Or might the nurturing of a mother, even a forlorn one, have helped me get through my teen years… and later as a young adult trying to find my way?"

He stops abruptly, allowing for the flurry of questions to register. The tilt of his head suggests he isn't quite done. "It's impossible to know, of course," he says, returning to his normal speed and volume, "and the only time I stop to speculate is when we're together and talk about these things. One thing is certain, though…" He closes his eyes for an instant, and a hint of a smile crosses his lips, as if he's seeing the future. ". . . my life would've been different. First off," he skips a beat, his head rotating toward David, "you and I would not have met. If, by chance, we did, who knows if we would've been friends at all or if it would've lasted only through high school graduation? Who knows?"

Rick shifts gears slightly. "JD, I was struck by something you wrote in an email recently. Something about the irony of our parents doing for us what they couldn't do for themselves. You recall?"

Staring trance-like at his closest friend, David scans his own increasingly faltering memory, an exercise that frustrates him terribly of late. "I hate when you do this," he says, feigning annoyance. "Why didn't you jot it down? Hmmm. I think we were talking about what we've learned from our mothers' suicides. I said something like, wouldn't it be the ultimate irony if our mothers, who couldn't save themselves, somehow in death passed on to their sons *the* prescription for overcoming life's inevitable disappointments? A prescription they never found in life? Did being forced to deal with the fallout of their suicides give us a different, and maybe a healthier, way of looking at and dealing with life's nastiest setbacks?"

"That's it," Rick confirms, tapping a finger at the side of his head. "A provocative thought, isn't it? That maybe what they passed on to us, ironically and unknowingly, of course, is a burning desire, or maybe a deep-down need, for friends . . . for friendship. So maybe something positive is possible from what has always seemed so one-sidedly negative. "

"I'd sure like to think so," Tom mumbles.

· · · · · · · · · · · · · · · · ·

"I want to return to Tom's acknowledgment," Rick insists, nodding in Tom's direction, "that, over time, your views of your dad – and his suicide – have changed. Which, it seems to me, may be an indication of how much you *yourself* have changed over time. You've said you're now more accepting, more forgiving, more understanding of your dad . . . and of yourself. Not an easy thing to do. Though I think it's true of all of us, at least somewhat."

Before anybody can respond or take off in another direction, Rick shifts his attention to Dennis, who's been doing more listening than contributing. "I'm curious, Denny. Do you think differently of your mom today than you did as a kid or as the young adult you were when she ended her life?"

Dennis is caught off-guard – and stares at nothing in particular at the other end of the restaurant, as if he might have missed the question. Just as Rick opens his mouth to repeat it, Dennis' eyes refocus, first on Rick, then on the other two. "It's been decades since my mother died," he declares, methodically refolding his cloth napkin into assorted geometric shapes without ever looking at his hands. "Sadly, I remember her as terribly troubled, a bundle of raw, undeveloped talent. I went through her papers and materials soon after the email exchange that introduced me to both of you" – he glances at Rick, then Tom – "and that poked me to reconsider her in light of the hard questions we were all struggling with. Made me ask myself how well I actually knew her."

"What'd you learn, if anything?" Tom instinctively slips into his professional journalist persona.

"Well, in a way – a good way, I think – I rediscovered a mother I'm not sure I ever really knew when she was alive. Much of her memorabilia, sketches, notes, newspaper clippings were from her last year or two of high school and first year or so of college. I saw clippings of her as the lead in community theatre, pages of beautiful pencil sketches she'd done and a couple of stories she'd written for school reflecting the difficult life on the prairie before the war."

Sipping his beer, Dennis' eyes seem to fog over. "It was as if I was seeing for the first time," he muses to his small audience, "remnants of her, and glimpses of her life, before marriage and children and . . ." The rest of us can imagine him pulling up memories and painting mind images of his mom, both the one he knew before her death and the one he never knew and discovered years after she was gone.

"Obviously," he adds in a melancholy postscript intended to capture the essence of his feelings and speculations, "I knew of these interests of hers growing up, but seeing these early sparks of her creativity so many years later saddened me that she didn't spend more time on them." He stops himself, as the impact of what he's just revealed about his mom, and himself, wells up. Then, stammering with emotion, he divulges something deeply intimate about himself in remembering his mom almost a lifetime after she left him. "I have all *this* in my heart now . . . and hope one day to write about her."

"Definitely, do that," David says softly, yet firmly – advising himself as well as Dennis. "For her. But most of all, for you."

· · · · · · · · · · · · · · · ·

The evening is winding down after hours of serious, emotionally demanding conversation, and Rick seizes an opportunity to lighten the mood. He picks up a clean spoon and waves it at Tom. Grinning sheepishly, Tom looks to David, who nods his understanding of what's going on. Suddenly, the mood around the table lightens, as Rick, Tom and David share playful sneers.

"You aren't thinking of stealing any of these tonight, are you, Tom?" Rick asks, fighting off the grin pushing at his lips.

Tom, David and Rick break into broad smiles, their memories tickled. At least one of us laughs aloud.

Dennis looks puzzled. So we explain.

From the time we met him, Tom was an irresistible candidate for playful teasing and practical jokes. Once we realized that about him, we exploited it mercilessly – to our delight and Tom's as well.

His warm-hearted personality, along with a deep-seated yearning for social interaction, infused Tom with just enough naiveté and vulnerability to be, at times, gullible and oblivious in the most endearing ways.

Not long after we met, the three of us attended a professional conference in Denver. At one point in the packed schedule of plenary sessions, cocktail receptions and how-to workshops, we found ourselves sharing a few downtime moments in a designated lounge. We were seated at a round, linen-draped banquet table, with Tom strategically situated between the two of us, nursing drinks and shooting the bull in our unbuttoned suit jackets and loosened ties, the required business uniform of the time.

Taking turns, one of us would draw Tom's attention with unbroken conversation while the other, positioned just outside his peripheral vision, deposited hotel-issue silverware – thick, heavy forks and spoons – into the outer pockets of Tom's sport coat, with chatty Tommy none the wiser. Before long, Tom's pockets were sagging and clinking whenever he moved or gestured, though he was still blissfully unaware.

With phase I of our prank completed, we exchanged nods just before standing up suddenly, startling Tom. "Dinner time," David said. "Let's go, Tommy." Ever ravenous, a bewildered Tom reflexively rose from his chair, instantly aware of the added weight on either side of him, which stopped him in his tracks. But before it fully registered with him, his pockets started jingling like a winning slot machine on the Vegas strip. All heads within earshot swiveled toward him, as it hit him that he was the source of the ruckus. He felt inside one of his overloaded pockets and the expression on his face went from out-and-out surprise – *"how did these things get in here?"* – to jovial discovery – *"Oh, man, you guys!"* – to amazement – *"I'm carrying enough silverware for a banquet!"*

Pulling silverware from one pocket and then the other, a fork followed by a spoon followed by a fork, a seemingly bottomless supply, Tom's naturally ruddy complexion grew redder and his smile wider – as the laughter all around him grew louder and more raucous. The night club act was on and his fans wanted more. We tried our best to remain impassive while the prank played out, but we could only hold it in for so long before belly laughs overtook us. But as hard as we laughed, Tom laughed even harder.

And Tom, humble and playful and a bit of a ham, instantly warmed to the impromptu standup routine, staying in "character" until he had fully emptied both pockets and piled the silverware into a heap for all to admire. Then, improvising – for his own delight and protection, no doubt – he checked the inside pockets of his sport coat. Just in case.

A year or two later, at another meeting, we managed to snag Tommy yet again with our arguably questionable sense of humor – this time with cut glass salt and pepper shakers. For him, it was as much fun as before, and he chortled with similar glee, at himself, at us, at life.

Times such as these – spontaneous, fun-loving, noteworthy – when protective barriers are lowered and true selves revealed, never fail to draw us closer.

Little could any of us know, or have even an inkling, in that playful moment in Denver how *much* closer the three of us would become some 15 years later, when we would stumble into a very different kind of moment – an extraordinary one – while shooting the breeze on an old wood bench by the shores of Lake Michigan.

Chapter XIII

. . . .

May 9-11, 2005

. . . .

From: **David**
To: Tommy, Dennis, Rick
Subject: *Seeking Answers*
Date: May 9, 2005

Predictably, my mother's shocking suicide triggered a cavern-size rift between the two sides of my family, complete with unrelenting finger-pointing and sweeping accusations of blame volleyed back and forth for years. Who did what to whom when? Who was right and who wasn't? Who really knew what happened? Who should I believe?

A byproduct of this family schism was that I was, not surprisingly, given conflicting interpretations of what happened to my mother and why, the circumstances of her enduring unhappiness, and why, at times, she felt deprived of all hope and saw no other way out than to swallow a bottle of pills or slash her wrists with one of my father's razor blades. The positive side of this scenario was that it forced me to seek my own best understanding of this woman I barely knew at 13, when she was suddenly gone from my life. I didn't realize it at the time, looking back now, but I guess I set out on my own "internal" investigation to discover who my mother really was and what propelled her to want to end her life before her time.

To be expected, my attempt to find that middle-ground truth, if you will, did not yield a definitive set of facts or circumstances or explanations that painted a clear, indisputable picture of my mother's sad life; however, while many questions still persist, and always will, I was able to add bits and pieces to my understanding, certainly more than anybody else was willing to tell me. Ultimately, by finding a few more pieces to the puzzle, I think I came to know her a little better, a little more intimately.

To the extent they would allow, I picked people's brains on how they perceived and remembered her, and the messy circumstances that defined my family life. Some family members were willing to talk candidly, like my Uncle Ben and Aunt Phyllis (my father's sister and her husband, who later became my proxy parents), and my mother's sister who was convinced that my father wore the black hat in the story. She seemed to have an unquenchable need to talk about her sister, who she loved and admired, but, unfortunately, never was able to reconcile that there were likely a host of causes that led to her sibling's heartbreaking suicide.

· · · · · · · · · · · · · · · · · ·

Toward this end, to get to know my mother in ways I never was able while she was alive, I found my way via several subway transfers to the mental hospital (that's what they were called back then) in the upper reaches of Manhattan where she had been a patient before she was released into her sister's care in Brooklyn, where, a few days later, she swallowed a lethal dose of sleeping pills she had cleverly squirreled away while in the care of the hospital staff. With all the chutzpah I could summon, I demanded that her doctors talk to me and tell me more about my mother's actual condition and why they thought it safe to have released her when they did.

After hours of waiting, resisting administrators' efforts to dismiss me as merely a grieving kid, and refusing to leave the hospital until somebody acceded to my request, one of her doctors – no doubt in defiance of legal counsel – agreed to give me a few minutes of his time. Recalling those washed out moments today, I was placated with the vaguest of information: She was severely troubled and depressed, she was a huge help to many other patients but couldn't help herself, and she was temporarily released because she seemed to be getting better in the hospital (an indicator, I've always thought, of her "acting" ability to fool her doctors and her fierce determination to take her life, which she'd been trying to do since she was an unhappy teenager). It wasn't much, and little that I didn't already know or suspect, but at least I walked away with something more than the pointless, biased pap I was getting from crestfallen family members who wanted to shield me from others' twisted versions of the "truth."

In small ways, what I learned that day allowed me to see her less through the teary eyes of a hurt child and more through those of a young man who needed to become aware of some of the darker aspects of the human psyche.

· · · · · · · · · · · · · · · · · ·

And so it went on for many years, this search of mine to "figure things out."

My father was never very forthcoming when I peppered him with questions he didn't want to hear, though he never outright refused to respond. Instead, he would avoid or play dumb, which he did quite adeptly. To humor or get rid of me, he might say he couldn't remember or "I did the best I could" or just shrug his shoulders and stare blankly at me.

I don't think he ever thought much more about any of it, and that's certainly true regarding the underlying causes and circumstances of his wife's baffling extreme depression. It was too much for him to see beyond the surface explanations, and maybe for a short while after, too painful to contemplate.

His innate emotional weakness, I came to realize, was a constant that insulated him from his own ineptness and others' demands of him. It was one of the reasons, if not the overriding one, he was never able to give my mother the kind of support or guidance she needed from a husband. That die was cast from the moment they decided to marry, I think now.

Sorry to have gone on way too long, guys. But I blame Tommy and Denny for opening up their hearts and souls (and thank them too).

Shalom . . . David

Hello, mates, it's the Kiwi-kid with more thoughts and feelings!

I received your latest email, Davey, and I was touched by the poignant account of your mom's death, which unleashed in me a river of emotions. The pain is still raw, the smoldering anger persists – just like your search to find out who your Mom was and why she took her life. The doctors, your Dad or other members of the family were, for a variety of reasons, unable or unwilling to give you straight answers to so many troubling questions.

My Sister

I'll address the questions Davey asked on the phone recently about sibling reactions to the shocking event and how my sister and I worked through the trauma after Dad's burial. There's plenty to say, but for now I can tell you our relationship has blossomed over the years since the brother she always thought of as the favored "first born" was, by my recollection, thrown off balance by Dad's suicide.

Father-Son Relationship

We were always a close, loving family, but parents have special feelings (so I'm told) about their first child. Dad and I had that special father-son relationship and my sister and Mom shared their uniquely precious bond that grew richer in the final years of my father's life while I was away from home for long periods – first at college, followed immediately by the military.

There are a couple of interesting, overlapping stories of relationships and how I turned to Dad for support in difficult times. But that's for another day. First, some reactions to what I've been reading from over the past week or so. On that pesky matter of embarrassment and the endless search for euphemisms, sidestepping the "s" word and what I think of as understandable, if unrealistic, denial. It seems ironic that when people like us most need to share this terrible grief, some of us have no one to turn to – or, more important, no one we're comfortable turning to – to discuss this most sensitive and painful time of our lives. Whether it's Dad, Mom, brother or sister, your minister or a very

close friend, I believe it's crucial we begin talking our way through the myriad emotions and feelings which can so quickly overwhelm us. Keep it bottled up inside and you've swept things under the rug temporarily, even as you start the clock on a time bomb ticking away
inside you.

The fallout from that emotional explosion can be crippling – or worse. As you cry out for help, you need a person (or people) you can talk to and confide in. But to open your heart and fully expose your feelings, trust is essential. The healing process takes time. You don't suddenly turn a switch that lights up a billboard with the words: *Tom Rediscovers Himself Years After Father Commits Suicide*. Indeed, years after Dad's death I wrestled with and was haunted by all those what ifs . . . the could, should and would of a life he'd abandoned . . . until I was ready to scream. And this, despite some intense and positive talks with Mom and members of our family.

Emotional Reactions

I weaved in and out of periods of depression, spent too much time alone and actually contemplated the unthinkable after my college sweetheart and first love made that other dreadful phone call to Hawaii, telling me she was going to marry someone else. I can still hear the love in her voice, and heart, during our tearful conversation. But this young woman who gave my life new meaning could no longer find the young man she'd so passionately loved. I'd become a shell of
my former self, withdrawn and non-committal to the very person who made me come alive.

Once again, my world had been turned upside down . . . why go on without the love of my life? Of course, I wouldn't have believed anyone who said, "Don't despair, Tom, you'll see her, talk with her again and write to her in years to come."

And Then There Were Three

It's strange, Dennis, how life often comes full circle. Gradually, with the right people around you, the healing process begins.

It's because of people like Dad, my first love, my loving wife and no more than a dozen very dear and special friends like Rick and Davey that prompt you to gradually reconnect with people. But why did it take the three of us so many years to discover we shared such a life-altering experience? That sunny afternoon when Davey, Rick and I sat on a bench along the shore of Lake

Michigan is etched in my memory forever.

With Chicago's skyline as a sparkling backdrop on this dazzling day, the three of us talked about many things. I think I said something about how my father often "escaped" to Chicago during those long periods away from home. One thing led to another and, before long, three close friends shared the most intimate of thoughts, let their feelings roam and, speaking for myself, felt an easing of pain through shared grief as we remembered some things that, when alone, we'd rather forget . . . or at least not talk about.

What was it about that day? Why did it take us that long to speak, listen and discover that each of us had lived through the same tragic event? One reason, as Davey has pointed out, is that it's just not your usual conversation starter, even among three people who have been close friends for many years. It has to come up in conversation, or else it lies buried, chewing you up inside, until you decide to give it the time of day.

This morning I took a long, close look at the three-panel frame on the dresser in our bedroom. The photos were taken of Dad and me sitting side-by-side in front of the Christmas tree at our three different houses in Albion over the years. What started as a single photo in December, 1946, when I was three, became a sort of family tradition with similar poses struck in 1956 and 1966 – Dad's last Christmas as it turned out. As I held the frame in my hands today, I cried quietly and yearned for at least one more photograph.

Yet it's strange . . . for all my genuine sorrow and deep love for Dad, this is the most I've thought about and talked about him since that mind-blowing day on the bench with Rick and Davey in Chicago in 1999. The danger in not talking about Dad's suicide is that an otherwise handsome, caring and loving father gets lost in all kinds of mental and emotional clutter. I owe Dad far more than that. He's already a ghost of Christmas past; I can't let that happen again, in the present or the future.

Enough for now, my friends,

Tom

From: **David**
To: Tom
cc: Rick, Dennis
Subject: *Trying to Remember*
Date: May 11, 2005

Tommy, you wrote poignantly of the Christmas tree photographs of you and your Dad in 1946, 1956 and 1966 and how meaningful reminders they are to you of what was, and what wasn't, after he took his life.

Tough to remember the best of times, without some sadness, knowing that your parent chose to end a life that forever removed the possibility of recapturing more of those times. How could a parent want to prematurely take himself/ herself away from the children they brought into this world with all the love and hope that comes with new life and new beginnings? Where along the road of life do they stray from the path they created?

I understand the fear of "losing" someone close yet again by allowing him, or her, to fade from memory. However inevitable that is. Similarly, yet differently too, I've lost touch with my few scattered memories of my mother . . . because I can't remember the sound of her voice. And there's nothing left to remind me.

It was only a few years after her death that I lost all memory of her voice. Where had it gone? I could see her lips moving as she spoke to me, but the words were inaudible, muted, floating silently on the winds of time. And there were no audio tapes with her voice I could listen to. And now, there's no one left to even describe to me in words what her voice sounded like. When my Aunt Micki, her only sister, was alive, she loved telling me of my mother's exquisite melodic singing voice, and how it was good enough to go professional if she'd wanted to. But, my aunt always added with a hint of regret, she suffered from paralyzing stage fright and so only sang when she was alone, washing dishes or in the shower.

Those times must've been before she had children, because I don't ever recall my mother singing, or even humming. I realized some time ago that without an ability to evoke even a vague memory of the distinct sound of her voice, my mother slips into oblivion faster than she would otherwise. A voice, after all, makes a person unique, as you of all people should know, Tommy boy.

Which may explain my obsession with conducting audio-recorded interviews with many older family members. To capture their memories, of course. But just as importantly, to hold onto their voices.

And thinking about her this way triggers a flood of other memories of her, some vivid and detailed, some sketchy and muddled, some sad and disturbing, and even that rare, occasional happy one I dare never allow to evaporate with time.

If you'll indulge me one of those memories . . .

. . . .

Whenever I think about my mother, however sketchy those recollections have become, I recall her living a life of extremes, with little sense of what most of us would consider "normal." She was either high-high, ecstatically cheery about something that gave her momentary pleasure, a night out or an afternoon of Mahjong with her synagogue sisterhood friends. Or she was low-low, stretched out in pain (real or imagined) on the couch, immobile, sullen, unresponsive, dangerously depressed, clearly in distress. I never knew which version of her would show up each morning. Or afternoon. Or evening.

Sadly, the low-low mother was the one I came to expect as the norm.

My memories of her, I hate to admit, are almost all of low-low times, when she retreated to her bedroom behind a locked door or laid still as a statue on the living room couch, oblivious to me and my sister no matter how many times I asked, "Mommy, are you all right?" As unnerving as such times were, it was commonplace in our little house in Lancaster, CA, where the front yard consisted of a few prickly Joshua trees surrounded by thorny tumbleweeds that blew in from the dusty Mojave Desert. My mother, it seemed to me as a boy, was a prisoner to her unhappiness. When she became gloomy and uncommunicative, I imagined her being transported Star Trek-style to a faraway land where she found solace and peace of mind. I wished that for her, even though I knew it didn't include my sister and me.

I'm remembering now one of those infrequent high-high times. Remarkably, I was the cause.

She was a rare presence at my Little League games. She either didn't feel well or couldn't face contact with others. Plus, I don't think she was much of a baseball fan. On this day, as luck would have it, she was there, along with my little sister.

I think I was 11, and the catcher for the Forest Lumber Solons in the Monte Vista Little League, one of several leagues in Lancaster. It was a weekday, late afternoon, so a fierce wind was blowing non-stop, as it did around four just about every day in the high desert. The two small grandstands were sparsely occupied, as the game was between two losing teams. My Dad, who was the assistant coach of the team, wasn't there that day for reasons I don't remember.

Before that day, I'd never hit a home run in an official game.

In my first at bat, I caught an outside pitch flush and lined it low and hard to right center. Somehow, the ball cut through the unforgiving wind and eked over the low fence that blurted names of local merchants. I'm pretty sure my home run trot was excessively slow and my rubber cleats were at least a foot above the dirt base path.

But it was the second homer that was the memorable one. I can still see it unfolding as if in a slow-motion replay on ESPN's Sports Center, each moment and movement exaggerated and extended, as vivid today in my mind's eye as it was in real time then. The pitch was as big as a party balloon, impossible to miss. I swung reflexively and the ball was instantly ascending toward the heavens, a spinning white spheroid bound for the great beyond. But it was the strangest thing: my hands felt nothing. I saw the bat strike the ball, but I didn't feel it. No vibration, no pressure, no recoil. Nothing. I'm told by those who should know that such a rarity represents hitting perfection: horsehide and wood colliding at their mutual "sweet" spots in what the baseball gods regard as pure harmony.

We won the game, not that it matters. And for a few minutes I was the unlikely envy of teammates and competitors alike. In the next day's *Antelope Valley Ledger-Gazette*, the local newspaper I would later deliver after school, a one-column wide headline blared: "Pincus hits two homers as Solons win." My mother clipped the short article and gave it to me to hang beside my cherished black-and-white photos of Dodgers players taped to my bedroom wall.

But what meant more to me than the homers and the momentary glory they brought me was what happened after the game.

Even though it was a school night and eating out wasn't usually in the family budget (it was hand-to-mouth back then), my mother – feeling high-high and carefree – insisted we have a celebration dinner. And I, as the slugger of the hour, got to pick the place. That was easy: Barone's Pizza House. My school buddy, Gene Barone, worked there most nights helping at the family-owned restaurant, where the pizza was always crispy and ultra-cheesy. And as luck would have it, dinner was on the house once word spread of the occasion (I'm pretty sure Gene lobbied his Dad until he gave in).

I downed my share of slices and any unclaimed by my Mom and sister, savoring every bite while chewing at half my normal pace, trying to keep the moment from ending. A rare and wonderful moment when my mother seemed genuinely happy and unable to stop smiling.

If only I could recall more such moments.

Excuse me for babbling on longer than intended. But I couldn't help myself, Tommy, after your memories triggered my memories.

Appreciate it, by the way . . . Davey

Chapter XIV

....

August, 1967

....

New York, NY

. . . .

The two of us are in the Big Apple on a three-day holiday to reward ourselves for a summer of work after our freshman year of college.

David spent the last academic year at Long Beach State in Southern California, returning to Maryland for the summer. Pinching our few pennies, we leave the driving to Greyhound and plan to bunk at the old red brick YMCA building just beyond the heart of midtown Manhattan. Only there's a glitch.

Despite Rick's repeated squawks of concern about obtaining *guaranteed* accommodations, David insisted we needn't worry about reservations at that "out of the way" Y. Except we should have worried – as we discover on arrival shortly after dark when we are greeted at the front desk by a "No Rooms Available" sign. Ever since, Rick never misses a chance to remind his buddy of his *faux pas* that almost had us spending the night under a cardboard box in a dirty alley. Fortunately, David's after hours call to his startled but delighted grandmother in Brooklyn saves the day – and her grandson's shaky credibility. After a subway ride over the East River, we sleep on his grandparents' living room floor in their cozy three-room apartment – complete with a homemade breakfast included at no extra charge.

The next day we reserve a room at the rundown Y. It ain't the Ritz, but it's what we can afford and it's just a short walk from the fun and flashing lights of Broadway and Times Square.

We scarf down an overstuffed pastrami on rye dinner at Junior's or the Carnegie Deli and catch a just-released movie – *To Sir, With Love*, we think – in a once-stately, turn-of-the-century theater adjacent to Times Square. Then we pick up a sampler pack of cheap wine – Manischewitz – to sip, or guzzle. Not that we need it, but the alcohol further lubricates our drowsy midnight conversation.

"Have you ever wondered if your mother gave any thought to you . . ." – David's whispered voice suddenly floats through the darkness – ". . . y'know, how much she'd miss you, how much you'd miss her, your future . . . *after* she swallowed the pills and realized what she'd done?"

Suffocating heat envelops us as we lay on our backs, motionless, atop narrow twin beds – cots – squeezed into the sparsely furnished, closet-size room. There is no air conditioning or fan in the room, only one small window that's open but might as well not be.

We are in the throes of one of our patented soul sessions.

For a time, the impenetrable question, like so many others we can't stop asking ourselves and each other, hangs suspended on the muggy, motionless air stalled somewhere above us.

"Obviously, you have," Rick says with an edge of sarcasm, wanting to deflect the query or at least stall for time while he assesses his – and his sidekick's – actual state of mind.

"Okay. Yeah, I have. And you?"

Propping his head on an elbow, Rick faces David, who appears as an obscure outline, a ghostly figure, against the dim backlight snaking through the window. "In a way, I guess I have."

"What do you mean, 'in a way'?"

"A different question, that's all." Dropping onto his back, he stares up at the low ceiling.

After Rick volunteers nothing more, David becomes perturbed. "Such as?"

"Well, sometimes, late at night like now, I ask myself if, right after she took all the pills, she wished she could turn back the clock two or three minutes and, uh, somehow . . . *un*swallow them?"

All sounds of breathing halt, as the unnerving question paralyzes us both. The silence that follows is as stifling as the oppressive heat.

• • • • • • • • • • • • • • • •

Though they advertised "private" rooms for rent, the thin walls and misaligned doors can't hold back noises pushing in from the hallways – shouts, scuffles, drunken conversations – or the cacophony of city sounds drifting in from the frenetic streets – sirens, honking horns, garbage trucks.

"Do you think she did? I mean, wish she could've undone . . . her suicide?"

"Jeez, I don't know…" Rick sputters, running both hands through his thick, straight, dark brown hair several times. "But, well, I like to think so." His flat tone suggests otherwise.

"Me too," says David, sitting up on the far edge of his bed, his bare back to Rick. "Don't know how many hundreds of times I've wondered it . . . if, as she got drowsy, she felt any doubts or guilt?" Sniffling back tears, he's grateful for the obscurity of nighttime. "Or," he starts and stops, "was she so depressed… was she so determined to die… that she felt at peace knowing her pain was finally about to end?"

"Who knows, who knows…" Rick says, reflecting a frustration that only deepens with time. "Would either of us feel any differently today if we'd been able to read their minds in the moments just before death?" He takes a long, slow swig from the mini-bottle of black cherry Manischewitz, almost draining it. "If, if, if, if, if…" he spits out machine gun style.

During the early years of our friendship, our soul sessions, irrespective of blood-alcohol levels, were almost always triggered by one or more of the bewildering questions torturing us since our mothers ended their lives – and permanently altered ours. Why did they choose to escape altogether from everyone who loved and cared about them? Were they in such unbearable pain that they saw no alternative? It would seem obvious, but was it? What caused their pain? How did it destroy their will to live? Should David continue trying to reconcile with his weak-willed father? Should he seek ways of accommodating his father's jealous, needy, vindictive wife? What about Rick's uncomfortable, deteriorating home situation with his stern father and irrational stepmother? How could he deal with living in a house so fraught with discord? And so on and so on.

Flopping back on the flimsy bed, his face wedged into a pillow, Rick speaks out of the corner of his mouth. "I don't think you've ever told me how you found out about your mother." He rolls onto his back and slips his hands behind his head, creating a flesh pillow.

For the longest time, neither of us talks or moves, while David considers what to say or whether to say anything. Outside, from what sounds to be several blocks away, a cacophony of blaring, off-key sirens momentarily distracts us.

Then, without a prelude, David, his slightly slurred voice thick with emotion, begins remembering . . .

"Thinking about it now, I could swear it happened only yesterday. And I'm seeing it all unfold again, just as it did then, only now it's in super slow-motion. Though," he murmurs, staring blankly into the pitch blackness consuming the tiny room, "it really was several lifetimes ago.

"August 22, 1961… a Tuesday. It was hot and clammy… like today.

"From the moment I opened my eyes that morning, my stomach felt off… off in a way it'd never been before. Hard to describe. A gnawing sensation, maybe. Made me feel off-balance, unsettled, uncertain. Like a warning of something I couldn't put my finger on. Something awful. But awful how, I had no idea." He begins shaking his head, slowly at first, then faster as self-doubt arrives, as it always does. "Or did I?

"All day long, the feeling stuck with me, wouldn't let up. I couldn't eat, couldn't concentrate. It wasn't until many years later it dawned on me what the strange, troubling feeling was…"

His mouth dry as sawdust, David takes a slug of the overly sweet grape Manischewitz and immediately regrets it. "Oh," he grimaces, then coughs, "I hate this stuff," and caps the bottle.

"Dread," David says weakly. "The feeling was dread. Fear that something bad is coming or, as it turned out, had already happened but I didn't know it yet. Later that day I found out. Oh boy, did I. The first hint was when my grandfather, of all people, opened the front door at Aunt Phyllis and Uncle Ben's house in Brooklyn. Avenue L. My father, my sister and I had been living there temporarily.

"Anyway, Gramps wasn't supposed to be there. And besides, he never opens the door, it's always my grandmother. Also, whenever he first sees me, he always smiles. But not this time. His eyes were red and watery, like he'd been crying.

"The night before, my little sister and I slept over at my grandparents' apartment near Grand Army Plaza in Brooklyn. When we left there after lunch to go to the movies, my grandmother didn't say anything about seeing us later. So I'm baffled as hell when I see her standing there, wiping her eyes with a tissue. But as soon as she spots me, she shoves it into her apron pocket. This is when I know in my gut something's terribly wrong. The spasms in my belly spread to my throat. I could barely swallow."

Rick breaks in. "What about your sister? How's she reacting?"

"If she's picking up on anything, she doesn't let on," David remembers. "Not at first, anyway. Come to think of it, we've never discussed that day. Never. Funny though, I can't remember ever feeling closer to her or wanting more to protect her, than at that moment. That terrible, horrible, dreadful moment. Y'know what? Don't think I ever told her that. I should've . . . I really should've . . .

"That's when my father, Aunt and Unc come in from the kitchen," David goes on as if he never stopped, "all wearing grim faces. Aunt hugs my sister, then me, tight and long. I still remember the wetness of her tears rubbing off on my cheek."

David touches the side of his face, then peers wistfully at his fingertips. "But she wouldn't, or maybe couldn't, look me in the eye. Next thing I know, we're following my dad up the stairs to the second floor, with Unc tagging along. By now, I'm sensing this has something to do with my mother, who I haven't seen or spoken to in weeks. Not since I sat across from her in a dingy diner near the mental hospital she was in, somewhere in Manhattan. She'd been a patient there for a couple months. Since we came back to New York after a year in Miami. The plan was to stay with her mother until my father found a job.

"But our first morning in New York, she slashed both wrists with one of my father's razor blades."

"Oh, God," Rick murmurs.

Loud noises intrude from the hallway, and David stops talking. We hear incessant pounding on a door, then a gravelly, insistent voice saying, "Hey Charlie, open the damn door and lemme in, you faggot." Followed by more pounding. Then a squeaky door is pulled open slowly and a higher pitched voice shouts, "Shut the fuck up, Rooster, you retard. Ya wanna get us thrown outta here, or what. Did'ya get it? All of it? Get in here, man." The door slams shut, rattling flimsy doors and walls up and down the corridor, and then, mercifully, the lock clicks.

And silence returns.

"What happened after she slit her wrists?" Rick nudges his friend.

"I've tried to erase all memory of that day when, uh, when she tried to kill herself in her mother's house. But, of course, I can't. I'm still haunted by the sickening sight of my mother's blood on the bathroom floor – two puddles of it. I wasn't supposed to see it, but I did. Just minutes after the ambulance drove away with her in it. But I can't un-see it. As much as I wish I could."

"Was she unconscious?" Rick whispers.

"Don't know. Never saw her that morning."

"How bad was it?"

"Not as bad as she intended it to be," David snaps, overreacting. "Sorry. Old reflex." He steadies his breathing, which calms him. "Truth is, nobody ever told me what happened that day or why. I figured it out later, after she finally succeeded . . ."

"Terrible day," Rick empathizes.

"Yeah, it was. After her death, it hit me. That morning, when I saw her blood on the bathroom floor, was the beginning of the end of family life as I knew it. *Nothing* was ever the same again. I was never the same again. For the next few years, until I came to live with Aunt and Unc in Bowie and met you, my life was one nightmare after another, always on the run, bouncing from place to place, not fitting in anywhere . . . not knowing where I belonged."

Hearing himself say the words out loud – chilling words he'd only *thought* up to now – startles David, and catapults him back in time to that fitful period in his life that's as murky today as ever.

"Did you see your mom again before she . . ." Rick can't bring himself to say the s-word at this delicate moment. But he doesn't have to.

David swings his legs around the bed and plants his feet firmly on the floor, facing Rick's bed. While Rick can't make out his friend's face in the inky darkness, he can hear his labored breathing.

"Once more . . . for less than an hour. We were all gathered in a shabby, matchbox of a diner just a block from the hospital. The place reeked of burning grease and musty tobacco. And it was so damn noisy, everybody shouting at the top of their lungs. Apparently – I think I learned this after she was gone – my mother somehow managed to talk her team of doctors into letting her out for a few hours to see her children. But only on condition that she stayed close to the hospital.

"The four of us were crammed into a lumpy leather booth, me and my sister on one side and my parents on the other. In the booth next to us were my other aunt – my mother's sister – and her husband, both looking as helpless and worried as I remember feeling. I can still see the anxious look on my aunt's face, as if . . ." – David's voice trails off to a trickle – ". . . and the streams of mascara tears running down both cheeks. That usually would've embarrassed her, but not . . . not that day."

David is suddenly exhausted, a washed-out dish rag. He's drenched in his own sweat, his glistening face barely visible to Rick in the faint bits of light sneaking through the window.

"Take it easy," Rick says. "You don't have to do this, y'know."

David shakes his head stubbornly. "No, no, I do . . ." – he gulps for air – ". . . I do."

"Pace yourself, then, okay? It's like the tropics in here."

David nods dismissively. "My mother looked the same," he says flatly, "except for her pale face and bloodshot eyes. But the truth is, I hardly recognized her as *my* mother. She was fidgety and distracted, chain smoking Winstons. Her eyes kept darting every which way, like she didn't trust anybody or thought she was being followed. Not once did she look directly at my sister or me, or talk to us about anything we could understand about the madness going on around us. Even so, I couldn't take my eyes off her, not with all the alarms going off in my head. She talked non-stop, faster and faster, like a runaway train. She seemed obsessed."

"Obsessed? With what?" Rick asks.

"She couldn't stop worrying about, uh . . . about, well, *everything*. Money mostly. My father's lousy job prospects. Where we would live and how they'd pay for it. Who would cover her hospital bills.

"I always wondered why we left New York in the first place, and then I couldn't figure out why we came back five years later. Eventually, though, with Unc's help, I figured it out. Enough of it anyway to feel less in the dark. We left New York so she could escape her worst demons – like her relationship with her mother, who she couldn't live with or, I guess, without. Then when things didn't work out in Miami, my father's job mostly, they may've felt New York was their only choice left . . . a bad choice my mother realized the moment she got there. One she couldn't live through again. But I didn't understand any of that until after her funeral.

"She was agitated with everything and everybody. With the past, the present, the future. I remember thinking how hopeless she sounded . . . she'd given up believing that things – that *she* – could ever get better. I guess by then she just wanted more than anything for it to end once and for all . . ." David's voice falters into a soft whimper as the realization of his mother's inescapable plight overtakes him all over again.

Squinting, Rick tries to make out David's strained face in the black of night. No matter, he can easily imagine it. He sits upright on his bed and crosses his legs in a yoga-like position, thinking. Leaning closer to his needy friend, he says, just above a whisper, "She had to believe all was lost, hopeless beyond repair . . . *right?*" David nods, barely. "They, both our mothers, had to believe that to do what they did . . . *right?* Nothing else makes sense . . . *right?*"

David nods again, wanting to convince himself. But a moment later, his chin drops to his chest. Then he twists the cap off the last of the wine samplers, a thick, sugary blackberry, and downs a long swig that sends him into a coughing jag.

"Oh, jeez, I hate this stuff," he rasps. "Tastes like medicine." He offers the half empty bottle to Rick. "Here, your turn."

Reluctantly, Rick accepts it with both hands. "I don't know about that, after such a ringing endorsement . . ."

"Medicine's good for you," David counters, between coughs, "*right?*"

We share a quick laugh, before going quiet and disappearing into our own memories of women we hardly knew before they were gone from our lives.

"I don't know why anybody ordered food that day," David blurts, returning to the crowded, smoky street diner where he heard his mother's voice for the last time, "because it just sat there, getting cold, nobody with the slightest appetite. I didn't fully realize it then, but it was really plain as day what was happening to my mother – even to me, a dumb, know-nothing kid then, barely 13, who hadn't yet connected any of the dots forming the picture of my parents' broken life together. I could see how deeply troubled Mommy was. How detached from reality she was. Hell, she couldn't even find reasons enough to want to live and be with her children." David pauses, and waits. After a few seconds pass, an odd-sounding snort gushes up from deep inside him. "Oh lord, I just thought of this. The last time I saw my mother was also, crazy as it sounds . . . the first time I saw her. *Really* saw her. As she was, not as I thought she was supposed to be."

A welcome silence descends upon the room, for what now seems longer than it probably was. "Just before I hugged her good-bye, when she cried like a baby and begged my father for more time," David revives his monologue, his tone of voice more roused now, "I remember feeling this pull to snap a mental photograph of her. She seemed so vulnerable, so helpless, so worn down by her struggle to, uh . . . to stay or go, to live or die. Something inside me, something psychic or cosmic or mystic, something I still can't explain, was screaming at me: *you might never see her again.*" Closing his eyes, David taps his right ear several times. "I can still hear the words, just as I did back then."

"I wonder," Rick says, a bit timidly, "if your mom was thinking the same thing about you and your sister."

David manages a flimsy smile. "I've wondered that, too, but –"

"But who knows," Rick finishes the brutal thought, now with us for life.

David's mind jumps back to the day his mother died, and somehow Rick follows the mental U-turn.

"My father led me, my sister and Unc upstairs. We went into my aunt and uncle's bedroom and closed the door," David says. "We each took a spot on the big bed, sitting or leaning on an elbow, forming a loose circle. Then, for the longest time, my father stared into his hands and didn't say anything. Neither did anybody else. Finally, after I'm not sure how long, he says, not looking at me or my sister, 'Remember what happened to Mommy in California?' And that's all he says. What the hell did he mean? My mind was whirling with the possibilities. My first thought went to her constant back pain, the surgery she had, and how much of her existence was spent stretched out on the living room couch as a semi-invalid. But that couldn't be it. Could it?

"My second thought shot back to the night a couple years earlier when my skinny father used a screwdriver to wedge open the locked front door of our house in Lancaster. My mother was home but didn't respond to his pounding and shouting,

'Gloria! Gloria! We're all here, let us in!' I can still hear him screaming her name, and my heart still jumps when I do. She'd left the three of us at my father's weekly bowling league, claiming a headache. And then, an hour later, my sister and I were watching her being rushed out of the house on a stretcher, unconscious and white as a sheet, with the ambulance guys furiously pounding her chest. I was told the next day that the bottle of pills she swallowed was pumped from her stomach just minutes before she would've gotten her wish. A wish of hers since she was 16."

Breathing hard, his chest heaving slightly, David's face and hair are soaked with sweat. He peers toward Rick's bed, trance-like, and wipes away a line of perspiration beads teetering just above his upper lip.

"But eventually . . ." his eyes flutter, then close, "she got what she wished for."

Seconds later, Rick's hushed voice startles him. "What'd your dad tell you happened after she left the bowling alley?"

David laughs softly, nervously. "He told me Mommy was really tired and *accidentally* – that's the word he used – took more sleeping pills than she needed."

"My dad told us pretty much the same thing," Rick cuts in. "That she didn't mean to. That it was an accident. Maybe he didn't want to believe it himself. That Mom committed suicide. But I'm sure he knew. He must have."

"Well, at first," David picks up where he left off, "I accepted that lame explanation, probably because I wanted it to be true. But soon after, I think I began confronting the God's honest truth, though not fully. Not yet. How could I accept the idea that my mother – *my mother!* – really wanted to kill herself? To leave us? Deep down, I knew the truth but I needed to hear my father say it."

Rick hears David gulp stiffly, almost as if he's trying to swallow his emotions. Wanting to say something but not sure what, Rick senses it's one of those times to just wait.

After a few seconds, David is back, his voice less shaky. "But he couldn't. It wasn't in him. He would do just about anything to avoid dealing with unpleasantness. Whatever words he used after that . . . well, we understood that Mommy was gone, forever. What I do remember is that he never uttered the words *death* or *suicide* that day or any day after. Purposely or not, I can only guess.

"I cried softly, and so did my sister, as the sickening reality of it all sunk in. I felt an emptiness crawl inside me. I didn't know it then, but would soon, that the instant my mother's heart stopped beating our lives changed in ways we wouldn't fully comprehend for years to come, if we ever did. Unc understood this but my father didn't. Or couldn't. He suffered a terrible loss, maybe the worst, but he may've also been unconsciously relieved to be free of a suicidal wife he never understood or knew how to help – and who he was planning to divorce, another shocker he dropped on me a few months later. He seemed to think in telling me that I'd see him as a hero rather than a weakling. So typical of him to misjudge how I'd react to that little bombshell.

"He didn't know how to comfort me or my sister, or counsel us, either then or afterwards when we were all just trying to feel our way through the darkness . . ." He coughs and clears his throat, then shuts his eyes tight, remembering the unforgettable. "That's when misery entered my life – and stayed way too long."

By now, we're both physically sapped and emotionally drained – from the long day, the oppressive heat, and the difficult retelling of a terrible tale whose ending we wish could be swapped with one from a children's fairy tale.

There's no more to say, at least not on this night.

Chapter XV

· ·

May 11, 2005

· ·

From: **Rick**
To: David, Tom, Dennis
Subject: *My Turn, Part I*
Date: May 11, 2005

Some images are etched deep in the mind with acid so caustic that they are always there, deeply imbedded yet near the surface at the same time. They are part of our DNA.

October 12, 1963. I am 14. My sister and I sit in the white Rambler station wagon waiting for my father to return. We're in a parking garage in downtown Dayton, Ohio, not far from our home in Kettering. Dad went into the adjacent hotel to pick up Mom, where she had spent a night or two – a short vacation away from the routine of the house and caring for the two of us, we were told.

My sister, then 9, and I had been to religious school at Temple Israel and this was a stop on the way home. As my sister grows impatient, I try to entertain her. Even reassure her when Mom and Dad aren't back within a few minutes. Nothing wrong, I tell her. More time passes. They probably had to finish putting her things in a bag and then stand in line to check out, I say. I distract her – and myself – with games and stories.

A stranger comes to the front of the car, just the other side of the metal barrier that keeps cars from hitting the wall. He shouts to us and confirms who we are. He says Dad is delayed a bit but will be here shortly.

Shortly turns into a long time. Again, I try to distract my sister.

And then, looking down the sloping garage floor, I see Dad, his head down, our rabbi by his side. I know immediately that something is terribly, tragically wrong. I burst into tears and scream from the bottom of my soul.

Few things could be as devastating as losing a parent while you are still a child – and particularly losing a parent to suicide. Knowing that your mother or father chose to die. To leave . . . *you*. Without a word. And not really understanding *why*.

I remember feeling that total sense of loss, feeling adrift, empty, numb. For at least a couple of years, I felt immersed in a dense fog. I emerged slowly. Very slowly.

I don't remember feeling ashamed – although, in truth, I didn't talk to many people about the cause of Mom's death, so maybe there was some embarrassment. As I mentioned in an earlier email, I know my father didn't want it known that Mom had killed herself. He even contacted an Air Force Reserve buddy who was editor of the *Dayton Daily News* to ask that her death notice or any published report of police activity not mention how she died.

As I understand it, it is common for children to blame themselves for a parent's suicide. I don't believe I have ever felt that it was my fault or that I contributed to her feeling of desperation; in this sense, I may differ from the three of you.

I don't know what prompted Mom to take her life. I remember only short snippets of her and the part of our lives we shared. I wish I could recall more. I have a picture of her in my head, but – as David and I have discussed before and as he noted in one of his emails – can't hear the sound of her voice.

I can imagine a combination of forces that contributed to her deep sadness and, perhaps, made her feel helpless. She and Dad had each lived all their lives in New York when they married. He soon shipped off to pilot training and then to Europe during World War II. She was close to her mother – a controlling woman whose small physical stature was deceptive – and to her two sisters, both younger than she. Mom gave birth to my brother on VE day (1945), and Dad came home not long thereafter. They remained in New York while Dad went to NYU for his Bachelor's degree at night and worked during the days.

I was born in 1949 and, almost immediately, Dad moved us to take a new job. It wasn't far – I believe we moved to Long Island – but it was the first time Mom and Dad had lived out of the Big Apple (other than Dad during his World War II Army Air Corps service), and it was the first time Mom was away from her family.

Subsequent job changes and transfers meant uprooting the household, and the biggest burden fell on Mom. We were variously in Long Island (two different times), Pennsylvania, and Ohio (three times). Mom was introverted and insecure, and though she made a few friends, I don't recall her having any close friendships. And she never learned to drive. In New York, she didn't need to. Later, her aborted attempts at learning how to drive ended in frustration. Dad, not the most patient of men, tried teaching her. So she was wholly dependent on Dad or acquaintances to get out of the house.

Taking care of three kids couldn't have been easy, especially with no support mechanism – family or friends – and limited mobility. No one to pitch in to care for me, my brother and sister. No friends to escape with to shop or go to a movie. No extended family to complain to or celebrate with. Even long-distance phone calls were limited because, as I'm sure each of you remembers, they cost extra and the family had limited financial resources. Dad was always very cautious with money; I suspect that also put pressure on Mom.

Their marriage was, for the most part, a traditional one: Dad was the bread winner, Mom was the stay-at-home mother and housekeeper. Dad took his role very seriously. He worked hard and was intent on providing for his family. We were never well off, but never poor, either. We had moved from lower-middle-class to solid middle-class by the time Mom died.

Dad could be quite stern, even cruel at times, and he could have angry outbursts. I don't remember him ever striking Mom, but his corporal punishment left hand-shaped welts on the backs of my legs more than once. Even more withering at times was the anger in his voice, his scathing comments, and his condescending tone.

This was the cloistered environment in which my mother lived when she decided to take her life only a week before her 40th birthday. As far as I know, it was her only attempt. I don't recall her being "depressed," though I doubt I would have recognized it at that age. And whatever her emotional state, it was normal to me. It was the only household I knew. I didn't spend much time in other kids' homes; didn't see their parents interact with them or each other. I do remember being in bed one night not long before she died and hearing her say plaintively to my Dad, "Mark, I feel sick. Drunken sick." Even in hindsight, I have no context for that statement, but it does stick in my mind.

In fairness, I also remember tender moments between Mom and Dad. I have pictures in my head of them slow-dancing in the kitchen to a Frank Sinatra record; Mom sitting on Dad's lap in the living room chair; the two of them – or the whole family – going out to dinner, a much rarer and special event then than it is now. A casual neighborhood steak place, with red vinyl booths and dim lighting, was one of Mom and Dad's favorites, and I remember going with them a couple of times. Those were special occasions! And I recall Mom and Dad closing the door to their bedroom for Saturday afternoon naps that I thought were "just naps" but may have been a bit more.

The tragedy of Mom's suicide was compounded by my maternal grandmother's reactions. She was adamant that she and her other two daughters would have nothing to do with my father. They wouldn't talk to him, wouldn't acknowledge him, would not "forgive" him.

My grandmother did come to my brother's wedding in 1969, six years after Mom's suicide. I remember being in her hotel room and pleading with her to reconsider her position, begging her to help put our family back together. This petite woman sat ramrod straight on the edge of the bed, fixed her eyes on the far wall, and repeated her promise never to forgive my father.

That was the end of any relationship I would have with the maternal side of the family, and the last time I would see any of them. My mother's two sisters were as loyal to their mother as I was to my father. The family tree was irrevocably severed – another reason to mourn.

I barely remember Mom's funeral, my mental fog was so thick. I have a picture of being in the limo, but that's about all. The children were not allowed to go to Mom's burial. I guess the adults were trying to protect us, but I think that was a big mistake. Years later, while I was still living in Princeton, my sister came to visit and the two of us drove to Mom's cemetery plot. There was Mom's headstone, next to her father's (who died the year my sister was born), her mother's, and other family members. The two of us talked a bit, remembering bits and pieces of what Mom was like and of our lives before and after she killed herself. Then we were quiet. Thinking. Praying in our own ways. Being sad, and reflective, together. Sharing the greatest sorrow of our lives, mostly in silence.

In the months after Mom's death, my sister and I grew much closer. My older brother was away at school – his freshman year at Miami University in Oxford, Ohio – when Mom killed herself. So it was my sister and me and Dad. I remember going to Temple Israel for religious school. If Dad dropped us off early, my sister and I would go into the sanctuary, dark except for the Eternal Light, and just sit there.

Curiously, part of my reaction at the time was concern for Dad and my sister – that is, for filling part of the void that Mom left. I remember taking on some of the household chores and being very worried about the small nuclear family that was left at home. Maybe focusing on them and on housework helped occupy me, made me feel like I was doing something, and distracted me from the pain of Mom's death.

I can only imagine how Dad felt. He was always stoic – to a fault – so he didn't outwardly express much emotion. But he must have felt great pain, a real void in his life and, in addition to the embarrassment evidenced by that call to the newspaper editor, undoubtedly carried guilt. That had to have been exacerbated by the blame my maternal grandmother thrust at Dad. I vividly remember her shrieking at him: "You killed my daughter! You killed my daughter!"

Pain on pain.

-- Rick

Chapter XVI

....

September, 1999

....

Luray, VA

. . . .

Rick's dad, Mark, passed away at the age of 76.

Mark started feeling tingling and numbness in his feet and legs 30 or 35 years before, when he was in his early or mid-40s. Initially, it was a mere annoyance he faced with his usual stoicism. The phenomenon – the symptoms were similar to multiple sclerosis, but MLS and ALS were ruled out – was never conclusively diagnosed and spread gradually. It forced him to use a cane, then confined him to a wheel chair, and ultimately put him full-time in a nursing facility near the retirement home he shared with his fourth wife in Luray, Virginia.

Eventually, unable to move his atrophied arms or legs, he became increasingly feeble and decreasingly conversant. A man long proud – and protective – of his independence and emotional strength was stripped of both by an ailment that could not be diagnosed or treated. As his son, who always sought his father's taciturn approval, Rick felt simultaneously compelled and reluctant to visit his dad in his waning days. Other than just being there with, and for, him a few days at a time, there was little he could do to relieve his father's pain or frustration, or slow the trajectory of his fatal illness.

. . . .

It is a hot, sticky, late summer weekend.

Rick is in the nursing home on one of his periodic weekend visits. The odor of stale urine mixed with antiseptic cleaning fluids permeates the hallways and rooms, offending the senses. He sits uncomfortably in a worn, vinyl-cushioned chair at his dad's bedside making small talk on subjects that used to interest Mark, such as the next presidential campaign or the Bill Clinton impeachment hearings. It has become increasingly challenging to get his dad to say more than a few words at a time. *Gunga Din*, one of Mark's favorite movies, plays on the TV, but at this point, it is mere background noise.

Rick checks his watch. It's late Sunday afternoon, time for him to begin the 90-minute drive back to Dulles for his flight home to Cleveland and work the next morning. Timing is already tight when he says goodbye, planting a light kiss on his dad's forehead. Then, as he reaches the doorway, he hears a weak voice call out: "Rick."

Startled, Rick turns toward the bed where his father lays motionless, eyes closed.

"I'm sorry," Mark rasps, barely audible. And nothing more.

"I was so surprised," Rick later tells David over the phone. "I didn't know what to say or if I should say anything. I acknowledged Dad's apology, but I was running late, so I didn't. I was so stunned that he talked at all, let alone that he expressed regret at, at . . . *who knows what* . . . at that particular moment. When I'm walking out the door. Now, of course, I wish I'd asked him, even if it meant missing my plane."

"Curious timing, certainly," notes David, "and it probably took every ounce of strength he had left to say the words." When Rick doesn't react, he asks the obvious question, "What do *you* think he was apologizing for?"

For several ticks of the clock, the only sound heard over the static-charged line is Rick's muted sigh. "I just don't know. Maybe he was sorry for being a burden, to me, to his other children, to his wife. For being in such a helpless condition, confined to a nursing home bed for whatever time he had left. Or that I had to see him that way. He prided himself on being his own man, self-sufficient, always in control. Yet here he is, unable to feed himself. Can't even hold a fork, let alone move his hand to his mouth . . ."

The friends share a meaningful silence to gather themselves. "My grandfather was like that at the end too," David recalls, clearing his throat of emotions. "A shell of the man he was before the stroke changed him into a man I barely recognized. When I'd get down in the dumps after seeing him deteriorate a little more, angry at such cruelty to a man so kind all his life, Aunt Phyllis would remind me to see him as he would want me to remember him, not as the frail stranger occupying his body now."

"And were you able to do that?"

David teeters between the truth and wanting to comfort his hurting friend. "Uh, that's a tough one. I sure tried, but it wasn't easy to do . . . certainly not when I had to see him suffering so, robbed of speech and mobility and all capability to care for himself. Later on, it helped me a lot."

"I think I understand," Rick says faintly, sniffling. "It's sad, David — and rips me up. I doubt he was ever very happy. Or happy for long. There was so much he wanted to do, but never got to . . . like travel after he retired. Spend time in the west. When he was a teenager, he'd study a subject each summer, research it in the library. One summer it was American Indians. He would've loved visiting the national and tribal parks out west. He was an Eagle Scout, Order of the Arrow. He liked camping and hiking when he was a Scout. He talked about doing that again. Who knows if he actually would've done it, but he was robbed of the chance."

As Rick's trembling voice trails off, David whispers, "Take it easy, Dickie. Don't read too much into your dad's apology. It may've been a far less momentous reference than you're thinking. Maybe he just wanted you to know how much he regretted not being a better conversationalist during your visits."

"Or maybe," Rick speculates further, beginning to recover, "he wished he'd been less harsh when we were growing up. Or maybe he was reflecting back on Mom's suicide . . ."

"Or maybe," David jumps in, "he was apologizing for not being the kind of father you and your sister and brother needed him to be. Who knows, maybe it was his way of confessing. Which he felt he needed to do while he still could . . . and wanted to do it to *you*."

Rick considers that possibility, but isn't convinced. "Maybe," he concedes, the doubt in his voice unmistakable. "Maybe it was."

"Ask him on your next visit," David suggests toward the end of their call.

"I should do that," Rick says, with a smidge of determination.

But, as fate would have it, a second chance was not to be.

· · · · · · · · · · · · · · · ·

In September, only a few weeks later, Rick and his wife, Ellen, make the trip from their home in suburban Cleveland to the nursing home.

His dad is on an IV drip, face gaunt and ashen gray, eyes closed and crusted over, mouth agape. Rick tells Ellen that his dad looks as if he were the model for artist Edvard Munch's *The Scream*.

As they stand at his bedside, each holding his hand, Mark breathes his last breath, a heavy rale followed by nothing.

. . . .

A few days later, David and Rick are on the phone as Rick struggles to finish the draft of the eulogy he will give at his father's memorial service.

David reminisces about times he remembers with Mark, some humorous, some serious, all vintage Mark. "Remember when we were thinking about starting Sunday Donuts," David prods, already grinning, "and your dad wanted us to consider the decision objectively, unemotionally, just as he would? He told us to draw a line down the middle of a piece of paper and then list the pros on one side and the cons on the other. And that if we did that, the *right* decision would majestically rise up from the paper before us?"

"Yup. Just like Dad. Analytical to the core. But he loved watching us start that business, do the planning, overcome problems and have some success. And I know he admired the deep friendship you and I built. In some ways, I think he was envious. He never had close friends."

"Too bad. Hey, been meaning to ask if you got to ask him about his 'I'm sorry' before . . . !"

Rick hesitates, his emotions already frayed. "Nope . . . regrettably."

David knows how that kind of regret can gnaw at one's soul, often for years, or lifetimes. "Perhaps it meant nothing at all," says David blandly, unconvincingly.

"Perhaps . . ." Rick says tentatively, cynically. "I wish I could believe that . . . I really do."

"So how's the eulogy coming?" David asks, switching subjects.

"It's tough to write and I know it'll be even tougher to give."

"Tough how? Finding the right words . . . or controlling your emotions?"

"Yes." We share an awkward laugh.

"I've probably made hundreds of presentations to clients and colleagues," Rick says, "and given scores of speeches. But this is different. Way different. And a lot harder."

Rick begins choking up, but quickly catches himself. "I loved Dad. But we had a complex relationship. You know, we never talked about Mom's suicide. I think that was a failing on both our parts. It's been 36 years since she died. It had to be rough on him to lose his wife, then have to face and continue raising three children who had suddenly lost their mother. But I can't stop wondering about how he *felt* about Mom, her family, himself, us kids, the past, the future – right after the suicide and later on. Wish I'd pressed him to open up, even a little . . . though I doubt he would've indulged me. My sister tried, to no avail. It wasn't in the male genes of his generation to show – or admit to – weakness or vulnerability, *especially* to his children.

"I know he tried to do the best he could," Rick continues, sparing his dad further criticism. "And I guess he did."

"You never talked with him about your mom's death? At all?"

"Nope. Never."

"Really?"

"Afraid so," Rick says.

"That's too bad. But I get it – yet wish I didn't. It was the same with me and my father," David says, his turn to confess a twinge of regret.

"One more thing we share . . . and wish we didn't."

· · · · · · · · · · · · · · · · ·

Rick steadies his emotions and begins reading his draft of the eulogy to David.

In it, he acknowledges his dad's stern, sometimes severe personality, but also remembers his lighter and more caring persona. And he shares a few humorous anecdotes. One pastime popular at the dinner table was making up odd, often disgusting, ice cream flavors – liver and onion brickle, for example. So for Mark's 60th birthday, Rick and his siblings concocted, then served, broccoli fudge swirl. Mark, who knew how to milk a moment, tasted it and proclaimed the concoction "not bad" in his minimalist manner – then downed two scoops.

David listens intently, offering suggestions when asked, but mostly he lets his best friend reflect on his dad's life, mourn his passing, and test ideas for his eulogy.

"It's pretty short," Rick says, unnecessarily apologetic, after he has finished reading the draft to David.

"Yeah, but that's a strength. It captures the true essence of the man. As tough as he could be to please at times, I doubt he's ever been prouder of his youngest son than he is right now."

"I'll cling to that thought at the funeral," Rick says in a scratchy voice.

"You said you hadn't come up with an ending yet. What're you thinking about?"

The line goes silent for several seconds. "I thought I'd end with a quotation," says Rick, his tone livelier now, "a tribute to Dad's Air Force days as a pilot in World War II and his love of flying. He was so young then, flying huge bombers before he had even learned to drive."

"What's it say?"

"It's from a poem called *High Flight*. Written by a guy named John Gillespie Magee. I want to say that Dad has 'slipped the surly bonds of earth . . . and touched the face of God.'"

"Nice . . . no, perfect."

Another era ended, another chapter closed.

Chapter XVII

....

May 13, 2005

....

From: **David**
To: Tom, Dennis, Rick
Subject: *Compounded Losses*
Date: May 13, 2005

Well, Dickie, I was hoping you'd weigh in pretty soon with your story, and so now you have – poignantly, articulately, insightfully, painstakingly.

And though much of what you shared about the day of your mother's suicide I've heard before, it seemed somehow new, and different, and much more sad and touching seeing your words in written form, as opposed to hearing them in the rush of conversation. No interruptions, no intruding thoughts, no surrounding noises – it's your words and recollections alone, isolated, unchanging.

I've known you most of my life, but now I know you better.

This process – this frank 4-way email exchange – is uncovering more than I ever imagined. It seems the four of us have already forged a special bond I strongly suspect is permanent, and unlike any other we're ever likely to have. I realized this as I immersed myself in your heart-rending monologue of the multiple ways your mother's suicide changed you. Yet, the scars you carry from that death, that irreplaceable loss, left a hole in your heart, as it has in all our hearts – a hole that can never be filled.

Opening our locked away souls to one another vividly illustrates how the echoes of our hurt and yearning to better understand reverberate through our words as we recall a nightmare we might wish we could forget, but is never more than a whispered reminder away. Rick, the scenario you and Dennis both lived through, where your mothers' families blamed your fathers for your mothers' suicides, was the identical scenario I experienced – and it took its own toll in hate, hurt, split loyalties, constant confusion for me and my sister, especially.

· · · · · · · · · · · · · · · · ·

A vivid case in point I'll never forget, a memory that still causes me to shiver with anger, was the moment when I first saw the wording on my mother's headstone at Montefiore Cemetery in Queens. The marker, which now sits unattended and overrun by weeds and surrounded by other neglected stones, was put up by my mother's family (paid for by my mother's mother) a year after her death, known as an "unveiling," in accordance with long-held Jewish tradition.

The short service was officiated by a free-lance "cemetery" rabbi hired on the spot to utter the appropriate prayers in Hebrew as fast as he could. After staring helplessly at the chiseled words that tore at my heart, I started hurrying out, determined to escape the farce I found myself in, only to be stopped by my uncle, my mother's only sister's husband. He pleaded with me to put aside my anger and tears which, he told me, he understood and shared (if he was being truthful or expedient, I never knew for sure, and I never asked him). In deference to him, a quiet and decent man I respected and loved, I reluctantly relented and came back to stand in silence until it was over (how else would I have gotten home?).

The words scored into the gravestone read: *"Beloved mother, daughter, and sister."* No mention of wife. It was as though that part of her existence, which encompassed almost half of her 34 years of unhappy life and produced my sister and me, never existed. As if her husband, my father, never existed.

Not sure I've ever gotten over that vindictive slight, that subtle act of hate and selfishness. How could I when I'm reminded of it whenever I visit, or even think of, her grave? I haven't gone there often, but when I have, reliving that day of the unveiling – and so many other unhappy days connected to it – has never failed to rekindle my anger and leave me perplexed and distressed, all over again.

Shalom . . . David

Chapter XVIII

....

August, 2011

....

Queens, NY

. . . .

O n this sweltering, sticky day, the 21st of the month, David returns to his
mother's grave in Montefiore Cemetery, an overcrowded, weather-worn Jewish
memorial park a stone's throw from LaGuardia Airport and Citi Field, home of the
Miracle Mets.

The pull on him to be there on this particular day is overpowering, irresistible. He'd
been feeling it for months, once he realized that it would mark the 50th anniversary
of his mother's death by suicide. He hadn't set foot in the cemetery, or even thought
about going there, in many years.

Why he had to be there now, beyond the obvious milestone, he didn't know. In
truth, being here in this hallowed place had always unnerved him. Beginning with
the day, a year after her death, when her headstone was unveiled during what would
have been her 35th year of life.

Accompanying him today are his wife, Karen, and cousin Rhonda (his mother's only
sister's only daughter, with whom he's always been close). Karen's been here once
before, in the early '70s, but it is Rhonda's first time (she was a toddler when her
aunt died).

In times past when David visited, he preferred coming alone. But today is different.

. . . .

T hey are huddled before Gloria Butensky Pincus' inconspicuous gravestone,
heads bowed slightly, thinking their own private thoughts of what was and
what should've been. The silence of the place gently washes over them, bringing to
each a heightened sense of togetherness and connection – to one another and to the
woman they have come to remember. After a short while, David places a small stone
atop his mother's headstone, a Jewish custom symbolizing the permanence of the

deceased's memory. Then he presses a palm over the etched lettering of his mother's name, closes his eyes tight and lets his hand linger on the sizzling stone, as if he can feel the tenderness of her touch in return.

Slowed by the baking midday sun, they begin shuffling toward the exit gate. When they pass David's paternal grandparents' graves, the markers small and flat and hidden from view by untended ground cover, he kneels above them and stares unblinking at their full names and the dates marking their births and deaths. Wiping away mingled tears and sweat, he turns gardener and pulls out the wild leaves concealing the stones and then brushes away bits of soil and other debris, bringing their names, and public note of their existence, back into clear view.

As they leave the overcrowded cemetery, a less uptight, more melancholy David decides to share one or two of his precious few happy memories of the woman he was just beginning to know when she left his life. Whether Karen or Rhonda had heard any of the recollections before (most likely), they nod and listen attentively anyway, and even ask a few innocuous questions to keep David remembering and talking, sensing his fear of losing touch with waning memories of the first woman in his life, who soon won't be remembered by anyone walking the earth.

· · · · · · · · · · · · · · · · ·

That evening, in the cool confines of Rhonda's home, David phones Rick, who naturally knew of his on-again, off-again plan to visit the cemetery. David's mixed emotions about whether it was a good or bad idea to visit the cemetery kept his plans uncertain even after he arrived in New York two days ago.

"So, did you go?" Rick blurts out the instant he hears David's voice. After listening to his friend's yo-yoing for weeks, he wasn't convinced David would go through with it.

First, a deep sigh. "Yeah, I did."

"And so . . . how'd you feel? How'd you react?"

David chuckles. "At first, I felt dumb as a door knob. I couldn't find it. Her headstone. I wandered up and down row after row, certain I knew where it was, but after a while one stone slab looked like every other one. Soon, I was sure I'd been transported into a Marx Brothers movie, running willy-nilly from room to room, getting nowhere."

Rick grins at the hilarious mental picture. "Understandable, Harpo," he says, muffling a laugh. "You never were good at directions. Doesn't everybody get lost in cemeteries? Give yourself a break – you hadn't been there in, what, 10 years at least."

"It was embarrassing as hell," David snaps back defensively. "Karen and Rhonda must've questioned my sanity, watching me chasing my tail, sweating like a pig in heat, while I'm reassuring them I'm getting closer to my mother's plot when just the opposite was happening. After half an hour or so of worsening frustration, with my head about to explode, Rhonda starts dialing the cemetery's administrative office for help when, lo and behold, the gods took pity on me and I stumbled upon it."

"Thank goodness," Rick says. "The climax to the story."

"It was, of course, nowhere near where I claimed it to be. Duh."

"An honest mistake, really . . ." Rick says as sincerely as he can muster. ". . . That is, for an old fart with a failing memory."

David laughs out loud, instantly disarmed by his buddy's cutting jibe, a common tactic in their relationship, particularly when a heavy mood needs lightening. "You're right, of course . . . uh, uh . . . who are you again?"

"Uh, I am, uh . . . I don't remember," Rick plays along. "Who am I?"

Now we chuckle together, one of those moments when laughter and tears seem a perfect match.

As we each refocus on the serious, Rick asks again, only softer and more insistently now, "What *did* you feel being at your mother's gravesite on this day, after all these years?"

"That I still want to scream – at my grandmother most of all – and run far away from that dishonest gravestone. But then I realized it doesn't really matter anymore. Not enough, anyway. If I'm really honest with myself, I'm not nearly as bothered by it as I used to be. And the fact that I'm not bothered as much – well, that bothers me. Time may dull emotions, but it can't rework personalities. Hell, some things can't be changed no matter what. Like the realization I had not too long ago that almost nobody's left who gives her life – or death – a passing thought."

"You do," Rick whispers.

David sighs deliberately, ruminating on the implications of Rick's apt reminder. "Yeah, once in a great while, but, well, y'know . . ." David's voice trails off.

We seem to be at a loss for words suddenly, a rarity with us. But what else is there to say? In any case, we need a short break to catch a breath and regather our thoughts . . .

"Have you forgiven your mother for wanting to go rather than stay?" Rick asks without a hint of judgment. "Have you forgiven your father for his mistakes and neglect? Have you forgiven yourself, that 13-year-old boy who knew virtually nothing of what was going on around him, for not being able to save his mother from her inner demons?"

Ten, 20, 30 seconds go by, with Rick's string of probing questions hanging over us. The only discernible sounds are periodic breaths and swallows.

"Have you?" David asks finally, gently as a feather.

Another prolonged pause lingers. The questions are as exasperating – and the answers as fleeting and unattainable – today as they were half a century ago.

"Forgiving . . ." Rick says, "is hard, but possible . . . *eventually*. Forgetting is impossible . . . *always*."

"True and true," David whispers back, though he sounds unconvinced. "But I wonder if it's *really* possible to ever forgive someone you love for killing herself when you still needed her?"

The pointed question hovers between us, untouched – and, in many ways, untouchable.

Some conversations never really end. Nor should they.

Chapter XIX

....

May 15-17, 2005

....

From: Rick
To: Tom, David, Dennis
Subject: My Turn, Part II
Date: May 15, 2005

My mother's suicide left me and my siblings trying to come to terms with her sudden absence from our life, but also – and in many ways just as emotionally wrenching – dealing with her unwelcome replacement.

It was only about a year after my mother's suicide that Dad remarried. I have no doubt that a big driver of his remarrying was loneliness. I'm equally sure that part of his motivation was to have someone to share the workload – particularly to take care of the house and kids. And I am certain that he also wanted us to have a mother. Unfortunately, his choice was far from perfect. And the way it was handled was far from ideal. Early on, this new person inserted in our lives wanted us to call her "Mom" – pretty insensitive to our still-recent loss – but I resisted. I don't recall my sister's reaction. Dad took his new wife's side.

In what I thought was a great gesture (and considerable concession), I relented, biting my lip as I did. At dinner one night, I referred to one of my mother's hats, making it an imperfect metaphor for the "Mom" moniker: "I guess," I said, "that it's one thing to keep the hat as a memory, but it doesn't mean you have to wear it all the time." Dad, never a sentimentalist, thought it was a ridiculous statement, so I felt silly and embarrassed when I was trying to say something nice.

The four of us moved from Kettering, Ohio, to Bowie, Maryland, as Dad transitioned from a civil service job to a position with a private think-tank in Washington, D.C., and my brother soon followed. My relationship with my step-mother had gone downhill, and none of us was getting along with her. She was variously childish and erratic, impulsive and irrational. I remember one time when she slapped me across the face. I don't recall what had made her so angry, but, shockingly, I slapped her back. Despite her pleadings that he step in and support her, Dad didn't do anything. He was disgusted with her, too, and knew she had acted inappropriately.

While all this was hard for me, it was tougher on my sister. She was nine when Mom died, so it had to be even more difficult for her to comprehend what had happened and why. What's more, she grew up without a positive female role model. Dad's new wife certainly wasn't one.

Dad's relationship with his second wife went downhill but he didn't want to initiate a divorce; an attorney warned of the financial consequences. So he thought that by freezing her out, she might initiate legal action. His grotesque notion was to eliminate, as much as possible, any conversation or interaction with her to make the situation uncomfortable, even unbearable, for her. Dad informed my sister and me of his plan and enlisted us as co-conspirators. Since we didn't have or want much interaction with our stepmother, we acceded. In retrospect, the scheme was extreme and underhanded, and involving the children in his plot seems quite unfair.

David and I met at some point during all this, discovered our common background, and became fast friends. I can't say how much that has meant to me over the past 40 (!!!!) years. It's saved me more than once.

I commuted to the University of Maryland, working part-time to help pay for school and supplement my scholarship. That didn't leave much time for me to be at home, so some of the pressure on me was alleviated. But that meant my sister bore a bigger share. Now, she was the only one Dad could interact with at home. It was grossly unreasonable of him to burden her with discussions of his marital problems, confiding in her as he might otherwise have confided in a spouse.

Dad and his wife never did split up. She was diagnosed with leukemia and died a few years later.

A sad end to a sad story.

My sister and I were extraordinarily close in the several years after Mom's death. But as we built different lives in different parts of the country, we became more distant and only communicated sporadically. That is, until a few years ago when, by coincidence, she dropped my brother and me an email about her memories of living in Kettering. That has prompted an exchange of emails between the two of us, reminiscing about living there and about Mom and Dad. We've become closer again.

After all, we share the unthinkable.

It is hard to separate all the factors that go into forming anyone's persona. Unquestionably, Mom's death had a profound effect on me, as did our series of moves, Dad's harsh and judgmental style, his strong sense of responsibility and emphasis on education, and the estrangement of half the family. Would I have been a different person if Mom hadn't killed herself? No doubt. But *how* would I have been different? It's a question I don't dwell on, but think about from time to time. David and I have pondered this unanswerable question many times, still hoping for revelations that are nowhere to be found.

I suspect that, among other things, Mom's death has given me perspective on other events. I suppose her suicide simultaneously toughened and softened me. After all, there aren't many things worse than losing a parent who chooses death over being your parent. So, as a result, it now takes a lot to shake my core. On the other hand, at times, especially in recent years, I find myself getting more emotional about some situations, particularly those that involve our kids and grandkids.

I wonder, too, whether Mom's death – the ultimate "leaving" – has influenced my interaction with people who leave me in other ways. Or are all the moves the family made through my childhood more influential? More likely, it's a combination of the two. I need to ponder this a bit further.

The fact is, I no longer think often about Mom or her suicide or what might have been. There are occasional reflective moments and a few mementoes. A brass menorah. Bamboo rimmed coasters with butterflies encased between two rounds of glass. A tarnished cigarette box. Some of these are gifts I gave Mom, or that my sister and I did; we sometimes shopped in a small oriental gift shop in a strip shopping center in Kettering, and Mom seemed thrilled by these tokens. Now they spark memories, a bit of melancholy. Introspection.

The friendship David and I have enjoyed for nearly four decades was forged when the two of us found out how much we had in common: both born in New York, both moved around, both Jewish and, more powerful than anything else, both children of mothers who decided they could not or would not live any longer. I am certain that, if fate had brought us together in another circumstance, he and I would have been friends even without that tragic commonality. But as each of you knows, there is an extraordinary bond among those of us who have experienced a parent's suicide. So there are times – as we did last year, sitting on a bench in front of Old Main, the original 19th century building of the University of Arkansas – when David and I step back and think and speculate, and wonder what might have been.

Tom and I have been friends for some 30 years. But as he noted in one of his emails, it wasn't until a few years ago on a bench in Chicago that he shared with us the horror of his suicide experience, losing his Dad, his closest friend. Maybe I should have known. Or maybe there's just something about sitting on benches.

Dennis, I've gotten to know you over the years through David. And now through your baring of the soul. Thank you.

As each of you has observed, writing about this horrible experience and its impact on us is nearly impossible. I've tried – not too successfully, I'm afraid – to express my feelings and share my observations as best I can. Nuances seem important. I don't want to be stereotyped or have my experiences and feelings generalized with others. That's why I've tried to point to some differences amid the many commonalities the four of us share. We are a fraternity by tragic happenstance.

President Kennedy was assassinated a month after Mom's death. Although I was already numbed by losing her and the way it happened, his murder drove the sharp feelings of despair into me deeper and in a way I don't think would have been the case if she had not committed suicide. The country was shocked and horrified. I felt as if life was falling apart all over again.

— Rick

From: David
To: Rick
cc: Tom, Dennis
Subject: Realizing the New Reality
Date: May 16, 2005

Dickie, reading your riveting reflections on your mother's suicide and how her absence altered your home life sparked a memory I hadn't summoned in decades. A memory I had never assigned much meaning to, until now . . .

· · · · · · · · · · · · · · · ·

My mother took her life in late August, shortly before I was due to start 8th grade.

We had left the beaches of Miami for the concrete of Brooklyn the previous June, so I found myself starting at a new – but very old – public elementary school. P.S. 99 was an outdated, boxy brick fortress with dimly lit hallways and stairwells that were natural echo chambers, and scratched up, undersized wooden desks bolted to the floor. Its saving grace was that it was just two short blocks from the drab second-floor apartment my father rented a few days after the funeral, around the corner from my aunt and uncle's house at 720 Avenue L, a few short blocks off congested Coney Island Avenue.

I'll never forget my first day at 99. Didn't know a soul. Felt alone, disoriented, apprehensive, and out of place in every respect.

And then came *the* conversation. Back then, as a confused, lost kid whose world had just been turned upside down, I thought of it as an awkward, meaningless but necessary conversation. But I realize differently now; it was, in truth, the moment when the harsh new reality reshaping my life clipped me with a sharp left cross I never saw coming.

The punch was delivered unknowingly by my home room teacher, Mrs. uh, uh, uh [I can see her face and her mouth moving, but I'm drawing a blank on her name], a caring woman who seemed to sense my discomfort and melancholy. She was asking me questions to complete some standard paperwork on the new kid – things like prior schools, courses taken, contact info, and parents' work status . . .

'our father do for a living?" asked Mrs. Uh.

"He's a salesman. Jewelry, I think."

"And what does your mother do?"

At first, I said nothing, because I didn't know what to say or how to say it.

After a few seconds lost in a whirl of distasteful and embarrassing potential responses I couldn't bring myself to say out loud, I heard myself mutter blankly, "She died."

"Oh, my, how terrible for you . . . uh, what was the cause?"

I opened my mouth, but nothing came out. Nobody had asked me that since it happened. She stared at me quizzically, waiting for an answer that didn't come. Then she smiled sweetly, comfortingly. "It's okay. You can tell me," Mrs. Uh said in the mellowest of voices, reminding me of my grandmother.

I still couldn't will myself to utter the word, afraid how I'd react. But I knew I had no choice. "Suicide," the illicit word slipped involuntarily from my lips, the sound of my own voice uttering it sent a cold shiver up and down my spine. I quickly looked away from Mrs. Uh, the thought of her shocked, sympathetic eyes on me simply unbearable.

She stared at me, trance-like, as if I'd suddenly turned to bright green. Is there an appropriate response to that damn word? Then she scribbled something – the word itself, I presumed – on the form and just gawked at it for the longest time.

After clearing her throat a few times, she covered her mouth with a silk handkerchief. "When?"

I bit my lip, before saying, "August twenty-first."

She seemed to look right through me, as if I now had turned to glass.

After an overly long hesitation, she murmured just above a whisper, as if not wanting to be overheard. "What year?"

I didn't want to say when; I couldn't. Because to actually say it, especially to a stranger, might make it real. *Really* real. I'd been doing a pretty good job of dodging the truth since her death, pushing it off to the sidelines of my consciousness, and my broken heart. But in that moment of clarity, reality cascaded down on me with avalanche force: My mother was gone. And she wasn't coming back.

"This year," I mumbled, still refusing to meet Mrs. Uh's syrupy gaze. "Two weeks ago," I added, unnecessarily (though I think I needed to hear myself say it).

Momentarily paralyzed, Mrs. Uh's face melted into a drippy-eyed puddle of pity and sympathy. I abhorred it; it made me feel worse, not better. Weaker, not stronger. Fragile as porcelain. And for that entire school year, that's how she looked at me. It's not what I needed, or wanted. But how could she know that at the time, when I had no idea myself?

Looking back, I've never doubted Mrs. Uh's compassion for me and my circumstances or her genuine desire to console a confused kid she knew had to be hurting. And though the revelation of what she unknowingly did for me has just struck me, I'll always be grateful to her for forcing me to voice and begin accepting what I preferred would remain silent, the stuff of fantasy.

Well, Dickie, I guess we'll never get out from under the weight of certain burdensome questions we carry with us. Questions that, at times, can be a good thing, like when they force to the surface understanding buried in the rubble of time for over 40 years.

Thanks, ol' friend, for prompting me to glimpse back and see things – and myself – differently. And more honestly.

— David

From: **Rick**
To: David, Dennis, Tom
Subject: *The Great Depression*
Date: May 17, 2005

David, now *you've* surprised me with a poignant story I'd not heard in our four decades of friendship.

I don't recall anything quite like what you described with Mrs. Uh after my mother died, although I do remember a neighbor across the street and one or two teachers being kind and sympathetic. I was numb enough, in enough of a fog, that I wouldn't have recognized if they were pitying or condescending.

Revelations about our parents' deaths are hard to come by. For me, one came about 30 years ago when I spent time with a psychiatrist. My first wife and I were struggling with issues that eventually resulted in the breakup of our marriage. I wanted to get to the heart of the matter quickly, but I also knew it was important to give the counselor background information that would help him understand who I am. If I recall correctly, I highlighted three specific things that greatly impacted my personality and my view of the world.

First, I noted, I was a vagabond. My family moved a great deal while I was growing up, and I went to 13 schools in 12 years (one of them twice). Although that exposed me to a lot and made me relatively adaptable, I had no roots anywhere.

Second, I described myself as a child of The Great Depression, even though I was born nearly a decade after the Depression ended. I said this because I believe the Depression so shaped my father's attitude toward life, work and money that it also filtered down to me. So I tended to be fairly conservative when it came to money (and, therefore, to spending), though not nearly as tight-fisted as Dad. I always saved some of my allowance or pay, no matter how little I earned, and watched expenses carefully.

And third, I explained that my mother had killed herself when I was 14. Unquestionably, that experience had a profound impact on me that is woven into the fabric of who I am, but I never blamed myself for her death. It was a very sad event that left a huge hole in me and my life, and changed my life forever in ways I don't even know.

The psychiatrist sat back in his chair and quickly observed what I had missed: "*That's* the great depression you are a child of."

— Rick

Chapter XX

....

Summer, 1985

....

Laguna Beach, CA

. . . .

When a friend is hurting and there's nothing tangible to be done to remove or lessen that hurt, the natural inclination is to try to offer up words of wisdom and consolation, even knowing none exist.

Sometimes, though, our mere presence – just being there, fully attentive – is enough. Sometimes, listening – taking in the words in silence while reading the gestures, facial expressions and feelings behind them – is all we really can hope to do.

And sometimes, it's all we *should* do.

. . . .

On a sun-drenched afternoon we cruise along the twisting PCH – that's Pacific Coast Highway for non-locals – that overlooks the rocky coast line rimming trendy Laguna Beach. It might appear as if we don't have a care in the world. If only that were so.

As he finished graduate school at The Ohio State University, Rick married and then served three years of active duty in the Air Force with assignments in New Hampshire and Germany. As his tours of duty concluded, he accepted a job offer in Washington, D.C. For about eight years, we both lived in Maryland once again. Then David and Karen, armed with shiny new doctorates, went west, accepting university professorships in Southern California.

On this picture-perfect day, Rick is on the West Coast seeking emotional support and mental clarity as he grapples with his complex and contradictory feelings about his disintegrating marriage. Months of lengthy long-distance phone talks with David ceased to suffice, so Rick flew cross-country for some extended face-to-face time with his best friend and confidant.

Unfortunately, reconciliation with his wife isn't appearing likely after more than a year apart.

As David drives, he prods Rick to reach deep within himself in search of the answers he needs to move on with his life. The more they talk, though, the more elusive those answers seem to be, a truth that only exasperates Rick all the more.

After a time, we park and stroll along a largely deserted stretch of protected, pristine beach near Laguna Beach's Crystal Cove reserve, shedding our shoes and socks, kneeling often to study unnoticed, energetic marine life that appears content swimming in circles in whirling tide pools. Distracted and seemingly alone with Nature, the conditions are perfect for straightforward, unvarnished talk – one of our patented soul sessions. It's been quite a while since our last one.

"You look terrible, y'know," David says in all seriousness.

"Can still can count on you for an encouraging word, I see."

"Well, you've got dark circles under your eyes. Like you haven't slept in a month."

"That's probably because I haven't. Sure feels like I haven't."

Rick trudges on a few yards ahead of David through the dense sand. He stops, squats down and scoops up a fistful of it, then watches it slip through his fingers until every grain has returned to the beach. Staring vacantly into his empty palm, his emotions starting to get the better of him, he confesses to David, "JD, when we got married, I thought it was forever."

"And now you don't?"

"I don't know. It's a muddle." Rick rises from his crouch to eye level with David again. "Dad asked me if we'd grown apart. I guess that's true. Hard to deny it, given what's happening, isn't it? But that seems too simplistic."

"You two seemed so happy, so in sync, for a long time. And then, suddenly, you weren't. What happened?"

"Wish I knew. But it wasn't sudden. It was gradual. I think at least part of it is that we were too deferential to each other. From things as mundane as where to go for dinner or what to do on the weekend. We'd defer to each other. A genuine attempt to be considerate at first. But somehow, deference became indifference. Or . . . maybe that's not it at all."

Clearly upset with himself, Rick turns away and gazes at the heaving Pacific, mesmerized by its beauty and predictable rhythms, seeking in its sheer vastness the understanding that has eluded him or, short of that, a little enlightenment.

Several steps behind, David hustles to catch up to his troubled friend.

"Are you saying you were each losing your identities?" David asks. "Or just losing touch?"

"Could be either. Or both. Or maybe I wasn't sensitive enough to what was going wrong. To her needs and feelings. To the needs of our relationship. I think I'm running out of ideas and moves to try to somehow make things better."

"You know it's not only on you, right? It's never only one person."

"I suppose. But I feel miserable about it."

"Can't blame you for that. You don't deserve it. She doesn't either. You think maybe it's time to accept that you've done all you can, however lousy that leaves you feeling now, and forgive yourself? Forgive her? Until you both do, you'll be stuck in place, like you seem to be now, unable to move forward with your lives . . . and be happy again."

"A lot easier said than done."

"Uh-huh. Always is. Especially now, before you've even taken the first step in a new direction. But you can do that. Because you've done it before. That is, accepted the impossibly hard reality that, as hard as it is to change, it's time you reconfigure your life . . . again." David glances at Rick and waits for him to do the same. "Know what I mean?"

Rick smiles faintly, then gives his friend a quick nod of resignation. "Maybe," he mumbles. "Just maybe."

Even before he arrived, Rick probably knew the marriage was over. Yet still he came, knowing he was coming to a safe haven where he could say anything, or nothing at all, and he'd be heard fairly and empathetically, and, in return, told truths he might find hard to swallow. And he knew they were coming from the person who knows him as no one else ever could.

· · · · · · · · · · · · · · · · ·

What Rick could not foresee during this difficult time was a soon-to-be second act that would change the tenor of his life story in the best of ways: a happy, fulfilling second marriage. About a year and a half later, he married Ellen, a vibrant and bright Kentucky woman who opened her heart and her family to him. Along with her came a strapping 15-year-old boy, precocious 7-year-old girl, and generic brown-and-white mixed breed dog. They wed as Rick accepted a new job with a management consulting firm in Princeton, New Jersey. It was a joyful and hopeful leap of faith for all of them.

"David," Rick jokes in one of their cross-country phone conversations shortly after he acquired his new family, "my new son is stronger than I am, my new daughter is smarter, and Fred the Wonder Dog is better looking."

"And you're surprised?" David chides.

"And, boy, these kids can drink a lot of milk."

"And you're surprised? Welcome to parenting, Dickie."

Chapter XXI

· ·

May 20-21, 2005

· ·

From: Tom
To: Rick
cc: David, Dennis
Subject: Response to My Turn
Date: May 20, 2005

Dear Rick,

It's about ten o'clock Friday night in Cleveland as I begin writing this. Thank you for recounting the tragic day when your mother took her life and how her suicide affected you and members of your family. Don't worry, guys, this isn't going to be another one of Tom's tomes! I just wanted to tell you, Dickie, what you had to say was well worth waiting for and gave me much to think about. I'm putting a few thoughts together this weekend, but I did want to make a couple quick points now (before I forget them!).

Nuance is everything. As you've mentioned, our individual reactions to that life-altering event, what led one of our parents to make the fateful decision and how various people did or didn't pick up the pieces, contain some similarities but, in other respects, are unique.

I wish that during our 30 or so years of friendship I might have gotten in on the talks you and Davey were having. As I said before, it takes a very special level of friendship, trust, love . . . and time before you share such emotions and deep feelings with another person.

In reading what you and Davey – and Dennis, whom I've taken a liking to in our exchange of emails – have discussed thus far, it would have been great to talk over so many things we've shared in the past week. At least we found that sunny bench in Chicago, but now more than ever I wish it had been years earlier. Which goes to the heart of another issue, how therapeutic and healing such a dialogue can be with the RIGHT people!

Oh, golly, I can hear the grumbles about those promises to keep it brief. A few parting thoughts for now, mates.

I heard a headline on TV last night which noted that three times as many men as women commit suicide in New Zealand. I'll get more info on this intriguing statistic and send it your way.

Finally, just before I received Rick's email, I got a note from a dear friend at the Voice of America informing me that one of our regular stringers, Ross Dunn, had died of stomach cancer at the age of 49. This fine reporter started out with the *Sydney Morning Herald*. In the coming years, his work would appear in the *London Times* and *Christian Science Monitor* and his reports broadcast worldwide on the Voice of America.

Ross was just a year older than my sister-in-law, Ann, and they both were cut down by cancer in the prime of their lives. In reading the comments of a journalist friend, Ross left behind his wife, a 6-year-old daughter and a baby son of seven months who will never know his Dad.

I'm not sure that adds anything to our dialogue, except perhaps to remind us how precious and fragile – even unfair – life can be, especially for a baby boy going on eight months young.

All the best,

Tommy

From: Rick
To: Tom
cc: Dennis, David
Subject: Sustaining Friendships
Date: May 21, 2005

Tom –

Your expression of heartfelt sadness and sense of loss over the passing of your former colleague, Ross, got me thinking about a gentleman – I use that term purposely – I got to know on an Alaskan cruise in the late '80s.

There were eight of us travelling together. David and Karen, and Ellen and I were joined by two other couples. Walter, the diminutive, lovable curmudgeon, who I met when he was one of David's fellow doctoral candidates, and his wife Joan; and Dacia and Rich, who worked with Karen as an accounting professor at the University of Southern California.

The eight of us made fast friends, forming instant bonds. At one in the morning, the sun barely below the horizon but still casting a glow, we sat in a hot tub at the ship's stern, soaking and soaking it all in, getting to know each other, talking and laughing.

We could not know then that only a few years later, Rich would be killed in a river rafting accident – a sport he loved and was skilled at – leaving Dacia and their little twin girls with only memories of him. And now Walter, 20 years our senior, is gone, too.

I am so grateful that we could share some precious time together. A posed photo of the eight of us all spruced up, taken by the ship's photographer on "formal" dinner night, has a prominent place in the gallery of friends and family in our home.

So I understand your feeling of loss for your VOA colleague and friend. Another life taken too early.

• • • • • • • • • • • • • • • • •

I realized after sending my last email that I was long-winded and rambling. I'm reminded of the quotation (Mark Twain, I think): "*If I'd had the time, I'd have written it shorter.*" And I certainly could have proofed it better.

Tom, our friendship started without the knowledge that we have a common horror in our lives. The fact that we learned about it only a few years ago doesn't change that friendship for better or worse. It does add texture and depth to an enduring relationship that has weathered periods of benign neglect. But even when we've not regularly been in touch, I've considered you my friend. And when we've connected again, or been able to visit in person, we pick up right where we left off.

I trust you know that I'll be there for you . . .

In my (too) long message, I said that I resist being stereotyped. Perhaps more to the point, I refuse to be defined by my mother's suicide. Nor are my friendships with David and you (and my new email connection with Dennis) defined by the tragedy we all experienced. We are each our own people, and I cherish every aspect of that notion.

Best wishes, my good friend. My love to you and to Jen. See you in Cleveland around Labor Day.

— Rick

Chapter XXII

....

October, 2000

....

Fayetteville, AR and Cleveland, OH

. . . .

"Oh, I keep forgetting to thank you for the 'get well' box of books you sent," David says during one of Rick's twice-a-day phone checks since David's return home after successful triple bypass heart surgery. "Arrived the day before yesterday, I think. Can't wait to wade in once I get my reading legs back. Attention span's still pretty off, like at the 5-year-old level."

"No hurry, the books are forever," Rick reassures him. "Just glad they got there. Time's on your side again . . . right?"

"I like the sound of those words, Dickie." David is sobbing softly as his emotions overtake him. That's happened frequently since he awoke from the complicated half-day surgery that not only rewires the arteries but one's emotional triggers as well, at least for a while. But he quickly catches himself. "Didn't mean to, uh . . . Your gift much appreciated, ol' friend. More than you know."

"It's nothing," pooh-poohs Rick, a bit unnerved by David's unexpected display of emotion. "Have you thumbed through any of them? It's no bother replacing any that don't appeal to you."

David needs a few moments to gather himself, clear his throat. "You went a little overboard, Dickie, don't you think?"

"Why? What do you mean?"

"One, maybe two, books would've been plenty, thoughtful and generous. But six? Barnes & Noble must've sent a limo for you. 'What other thousand-page tomes can we show you, Mr. Knapp?'"

Rick snickers. "Didn't realize . . ." he mumbles, baffled to think he'd done anything unusual or noteworthy – but he sees David's point. "I'd been waiting for a chance to do something to, uh, help, but there wasn't anything I could think of, so . . . So when I finally did think of something, I just, well, did . . ."

"I get it," David cuts in, immediately regretting his clumsy comeback to a thoughtful gesture. "If our positions were reversed and I was forced to just stand by quietly and watch you go through something as scary as heart surgery, I'd be crawling the walls, feeling helpless too. And when the time finally came when I could do something, I wouldn't hold back either."

"Not sure what I was thinking," Rick admits. "Maybe it was something like that."

"Emotional logic at work," David explains with a snicker. "If one good book can stoke the healing process, then imagine what six fat best-sellers can do to help my best friend."

Rick thinks about that before responding. "Whatever was behind it, I just know it felt like the right thing to do."

"It was very right," says David sincerely. Then, adding softly, "I love you too, Dickie."

Chapter XXIII

....

May 21-24, 2005

....

From: **David**
To: Rick, Tom, Dennis
Subject: *My Turn . . . Mine Too*
Date: May 21, 2005

I must echo Dickie's good words to Tommy about our friendships and the impact of our parents' suicides in shaping, or reshaping, us.

The kind of friendship Rick, Tom and I shared and created years ago drew us close, beyond just the professional ties we held; it was always more than the typical "professional" friendship we have with many others we work with, but then leave when we go home. With us, the personal quickly became intertwined with the professional, and eventually the professional became the caboose rather than the engine.

It's true, as Rick points out, that there have been times when we seemingly lost touch, but not really – time and circumstances merely got in the way for a while, perhaps. The bond has never vacillated, even when it slipped into hiding at times, just needing to be poked and prodded by one of us to reappear. Strange – and ironic – how life works sometimes. Even though Tommy moved to New Zealand, thousands of miles away, our communication has been, oddly enough, deeper and, at moments, more frequent. Thus, unexpectedly, the vast distance serves to draw us closer together, tightening the bond that connects us.

Perhaps we're just compensating for the vast geography between us. Or we've merely come to realize how much we truly value our friendships, and won't allow such obstacles as time or distance or any other factor to interfere. I'd like to think it's something like that.

Again, I hope who I am and how I've lived my life has not been defined by my mother's chosen method of death. I don't think it has. Yet, that said, I do think that we've each been considerably influenced and, to varying extents, molded and remolded by that singular event. Probably more than we are aware, or will allow ourselves to accept. In subtle, unseen and unspoken ways, that disturbingly traumatic experience is embedded in our souls and subconscious, at times tugging at our thought patterns and emotions as few other things can. Seems that much of what we've been writing about so far – our recollections and feelings – supports this notion.

I have been buoyed by our shared words because they really do prove Dickie's point: each of us has overcome what could have marked us, and taken us down, had we allowed it to. Instead, we've each been able to take half a step backwards and examine our emotions, and how we have been affected by the shattering loss of a parent by their own choice. In the end, our very existence today screams of how we've managed to use that loss, though not always easily, to catapult our lives to a better place.

I've thought for a long time now that my father's many failings – as a father, as a husband, as a man – instilled in me the determination to never be like him. To not repeat his mistakes. To push myself in a direction different than his, one of my choosing. Similarly, the negatives inherent in my mother's sad life have, ironically enough, impacted me positively. At times when I've felt lost and without hope, and the unwelcome thought of suicide visited me, I fought against it furiously, resisting the idea of ever standing in my mother's shadow, or doing to the people I love and care about what my mother did to me, my sister, and so many others across both sides of my family.

We are us, nobody else – products of our past, yes, but new creations, better than prior models, envisioning the future with discerning eyes we wish our parents had had when they needed them. If only.

· · · · · · · · · · · · · · · · ·

Talk about "if onlys," Dickie. One thought, or memory, almost always leads to another.

I'm now thinking about a huge "if only" that touched both our lives, mine in particular: Rich's untimely accidental death. Like you, thinking of him catapults me back to the deck of our cruise ship bound for Alaska –- Karen's and my first-ever cruise. Where I'm trading barbs and insults with you, ol' Walter and Rich. In my flashback, he's shivering in the cold wind in Bermuda shorts, sandals, and a sleeveless insulated parka, a sly smile on his face, practically begging for glib reactions to his incongruous attire. The California beach boy meets the cool of Alaska.

I love the mind picture you painted of our group of eight at one in the morning – the low, late night sun bathing us in a glow we "escapers" also felt on the inside – soon after sailing from Vancouver. There we were, blithely immersed in hot tubs "soaking, and soaking it all in," as you so aptly put it, as new bonds of friendship began crystallizing between the warm water and cold air.

At that point, I knew Rich only casually, as Karen's faculty colleague at USC's School of Accounting. She told me many times she thought Rich and I had the makings of true friends if only we opened ourselves to the possibility. But it took us a while to realize the truth of her belief. Sparked by our mutual passion for the Dodgers and Vin Scully, and our checkered childhoods (Rich was an orphan and adopted), we began to connect on a deeper level a few months after the cruise.

And then, just like that, it ended as suddenly as it began when he died trying to save a drowning friend while rafting in Arizona.

I felt a crushing loss. Our time as genuine friends was brief but sweet, and then bittersweet. And now it serves as a gloomy reminder that *bona fide* friendships don't come along every day and don't form overnight. They can't; they need time to take root before they can grow and bloom into something sturdy and durable. That's how it happened with Rich and me. Though I don't recall us ever saying it, I knew, and I'm pretty sure he did too, we had discovered something special and, presumably, long-lasting. Yet our slow-to-evolve friendship was snatched away in a terrible instant of an heroic effort gone bad.

But, as I've told myself over and over ever since, the time we did have –- well, it takes on more meaning every time I think about him.

So I say with all the hopefulness I can muster at this late (or early) hour, make today a happy one, in Cleveland, in Boulder, and in Titirangi.

— David

At first, I felt like the stranger in the group. Now I'll just call myself the newcomer. In any event, the personal stories you've shared have alternately chilled and inspired me. And sent me reeling emotionally.

I saved up each of your latest comments to be read and digested at once. All of them started my head going in different directions. Each of you has touched on themes or incidents that are so very close to my own experiences and thoughts.

You've all commented on the value of exploring these feelings we share rather than sitting on them and letting them fester. I heartily agree and am glad for this chance to explore neglected territory.

How have my feelings for my parents changed over the years? David asks us. For a long time, I blamed my mother for her alcohol-induced temperament in my late teens and for finally abandoning life. But I forgive her. I know that forgiveness is a must, the only route for ultimate peace. All our deceased parents did what they knew how to do, what life seemed to force them to do. If they didn't give us their best, didn't live out their parental duties, we can only lament and forgive. I have never visited my mother's grave in LA and think I will do that next time we're back in California. Even if just to say, "*I forgive you for leaving.*"

Sometimes we look for answers – Tom's "what ifs," and others. David writes about extreme desperateness and unhappiness. I've always thought of my mother as extremely lonely – that she had no one to turn to. Rick, your description of your mother as introverted, insecure, and lacking close friends sounded like my mother. Is that one of the reasons I cherish close friends above many other things in life? With the friends I have I could never be lonely enough to entertain the s-word, though I could tell you how I've imagined my own suicide.

Rick, your narrative sounded familiar in several physical and emotional/ psychological ways, in addition to what I've already mentioned. When I was young, we lived in Dayton. My sister was born there. My Dad was stationed at Wright-Pat. Yours too? I, too, am the product of a stoic, Air Force Dad and stay-at-home Mom. I, too, moved quite a bit as a child, though my elementary schooling at six schools in six cities in seven years can't top yours.

A suicide note? ". . . no more problems." My mother did not leave a note. I can't remember asking about that. But I must have. Rick, I'm not trying to put you or me in a stereotype or generalize the feelings, but the things we have in common stood out to me. All of our four narratives have shown both similarities and stark differences. We share the unthinkable, as you said. A tragic fraternity.

Would I have been a different person had my mother survived? Rick asks. In my case, I was older and my personality already formed. I think my mother's alcoholism did more to shape me than her suicide.

I've gone through my second round of reactions for you guys, not to prolong the cathartic agony (is that a contradiction?) but to air some things that have been tied up in an airless room for some time.

In a box in my garage are high school annuals, sketchbooks, letters and other items my mother left behind. My uncle received these when my maternal grandmother died a few years ago (at 98!). He gave me this box full of memories when my sister and I visited Minneapolis a year ago. At the time, I skimmed through the items and began to see a woman I didn't recognize.

When I flew home, the box went into the garage where it's been sitting for more than 12 months. I had planned to explore my mother and write about her and about my journey. You guys have given me the impetus to do that now. Thanks.

Tom, you and I have battled depression at times and you speak of now trying to jump-start life into high gear. I think you're at least half-way there, because in your last message you talk about how precious and fragile life is. Recognizing that, to me, is close to the secret of life.

As one of my favorite philosophers says, *"The secret to life is simply to appreciate and enjoy life."*

Thanks for letting me join the club.

— Dennis

From: **Rick**
To: Dennis
cc: David, Tom
Subject: *No Strangers Here*
Date: May 24, 2005

Dennis —

You're not a stranger. You weren't before, since David had talked about you often (and in glowing terms), and you certainly aren't now.

My Dad was at Wright-Pat – twice. The first time, he had been recalled to active duty during the Korean War. I was about 2 then. We returned to the Dayton area when Dad took a Civil Service job at Wright-Pat. It was during that period that Mom killed herself.

So were we there at the same time? About 1951 to 1953 on the first stint; about 1959 to 1964 on the second.

A sad fraternity, indeed. But given what each of us went through, I feel fortunate that there are others out there – friends – with whom to share.

— Rick

From: David
To: Dennis, Tommy, Dickie
Subject: Moving On . . . Always a Work in Progress
Date: May 24, 2005

Couldn't close out the day before telling you, Denny, how your reactions and insights touched me; it's clear how deeply you've thought about your mother's predicament and actions, and to points made by the other members of the club. Thanks for adding to this growing body of reflections.

You spoke of forgiving your mother for taking her life, and understanding that she did the best she could, given everything battering her, especially the alcoholism. I guess I've done that too, though I haven't thought about my mother in "forgiveness" terms in so long, I can't remember when, or if, I ever did; I wonder if that might be because she attempted suicide several times – two such times I recall the aftermath in unbearably vivid, slow-motion detail – before she ultimately succeeded.

It seemed that suicide was always her destiny, at least as she perceived it. I learned from one of her friends a year or so after her passing that one of her doctors in Lancaster, where we lived during my pre-teen years, predicted she would one day kill herself; apparently, he had never come across a patient as bound and determined to end her life as my mother, a desire she felt, and acted on, as far back as a teenager in Brooklyn (so I was told by her sister and others, after her death).

Whenever her depression reached the point of extreme hopelessness, I always believed she escaped to a place that only she knew of, a place where she was able to separate from life and others and the problems impinging on her, a place where she was free from everything and everybody, a place where, more than anything else, she could find the perfect version of herself that eluded her in life.

Have I forgiven her for taking my mother from me? I don't know. Is the decision to commit suicide a selfless or a selfish act? Or is it somehow a blending of both? Again, I don't know. And, if I'm bluntly honest with myself, I doubt I ever will. In my case, it's always been harder for me to forgive my father for his many shortcomings, some related to my mother and some to me and my sister. But it wasn't that long ago that I finally managed to forgive him – somewhat – for who he was and the many things he should've done but didn't, or couldn't.

I reached this point by accepting the sad and inescapable conclusion that he didn't possess the strength or intelligence to do anything other than what he did. I can't expect a weak, unseeing person to instantaneously become strong and insightful just because I want him to be.

And the loneliness that must've accompanied each of our parents at points along their path had to have worsened their depression, and extended their lost sense of belonging and being loved.   I know my mother was frequently depressed, unable to function, and I know she couldn't talk to my father about the things she struggled to come to terms with but couldn't. Her way of dealing, or not dealing, with her troubles was to escape to parties where she could be with others, be for a few minutes someone other than herself, and forget about all the troubles and disappointments that robbed her of any sense of self-worth.

When she couldn't flee home or herself, her ready alternative was to substitute hefty doses of pain medications. At such times, I barely recognized the mother I thought I knew.

I remember one night, I must've been 11 or 12, begging my parents not to leave me and my sister in the house alone, fearing a stalker or bogey man I was convinced I'd seen outside our front window the last time they had gone out (Genuine trepidation? A kid's forced fantasy? A cry for attention?). But my mother couldn't help herself and they went anyway, because she had to get out of the house, regardless of my agitated state of mind. One of several haunting times I can't seem to forget, though I've never stopped trying.

Anyway, boys, I sense that you may be feeling a bit emotionally spent from all our inner sanctum sharing, as I am too. But please continue reacting and disclosing if you're moved to do so.

Night, boys . . . David

P.S. Denny, if you're so inclined, I'd love to know how things go for you when you sift through the box of your mother's mementos.

Chapter XXIV

....

March, 2003

....

Death Valley, CA

. . . .

F riendship, though a seemingly simple notion, defies simple definitions.

It's a commonly used term that is wholly familiar sometimes while utterly mysterious at other times. Friendship doesn't mean the same thing to all. It has infinite sides and aspects, able to assume any number of forms and connotations, stretching from close to casual. Which is both a strength and a weakness that goes to the very heart of the meaning of true friendship.

Our lives are proof of what friendship is, and all it can be.

. . . .

O ver the last 30 years or so, the two of us have been extraordinarily fortunate to have formed a variety of one-on-one and group friendships beyond our own.

Often, quite naturally, a friend of one of us becomes a friend of the other until, as in several cases, clusters of friends meld into informal groups. Having evolved organically and gradually, they differ by mix of individuals, personalities, chemistry and focus, each sharing a common enthusiasm for the same meaningful "thing": A game, like baseball. A place, like Coney Island. A vocation, like communication. Or an avocation, like photography.

Of these groups, the one most closely resembling the sons of suicide – but without the inescapable, underlying tragedy – is the Four Foto Friends, as we've lightheartedly dubbed our little troupe of fellow photographers. The common denominator is the two of us; beyond that, the two groups play wholly different roles in our lives, rarely intersecting. Yet both are deeply meaningful to us.

. . . .

The two of us have dabbled in photography since the late '60s when we both lived in Maryland. At some point the hobby evolved into a passion, a creative outlet, a source of joy, and we sought opportunities to share our love of the photographic process with others.

In time, new friends entered the picture. Steve and then Bruce, initially both professional colleagues of David, were also dedicated photographers. Gradually, the four of us became friends, then good friends, and eventually a quartet who enjoyed landscape photography. Every other year or so, we follow our creative urges and convene for a week-long photography excursion, planned months in advance, into national parks and other picturesque locations. These forays have taken us to the wilds of Utah, Arizona, California, Oregon, Wyoming, Montana and Florida.

These trips serve multiple purposes: escape from everyday routines; time in magnificent places; the chance to indulge our common passion for photography; and, most important, time together sharing meals and homemade pie in local cafes, enduring long car rides, joyfully mangling lyrics to our favorite Western TV theme songs from the '50s and '60s, and solving knotty world problems.

Our close friendships with Steve and Bruce are based on common interests and experiences. Suicide is not among them, so it wasn't a subject of discussion. Still, these photo trips create a strong bond among the Four Foto Friends and continually broadened the deep friendship between the two of us.

. . . .

Our second outing as a foursome takes us into Southern California's desolate Death Valley National Park, where we expect the landscape to be barren, monochromatic and inhospitable. We discover, instead, surprising diversity and life in many forms, intermingled in a vibrant environment of raw, pristine beauty.

On this early spring morning, the expansive desert is cold and austere, and appears deserted. All ours. If there are other shivery souls out there, we don't see or hear them. The iconic rolling dunes, smoothed by the cleansing overnight winds, appear unspoiled and bursting with photographic promise.

This final morning of our extended visit epitomizes the joys, challenges, disappointments and satisfactions we experience during these adventures. As is typical, we are up and out before dawn, determined to position our cameras and tripods on Death Valley's towering dunes well before the sun's first rays. Dawn, like dusk, is a special time for photographers: it's when shadows are sharp, hues intense, and both are fleeting. In the near-darkness and ubiquitous quiet blanketing the desert just before daybreak, we struggle to climb steep dunes in pursuit of ideal vantage points, feet slipping continually, often swallowed up by the porous, shifting sand. Before long, we're all breathless from exertion – and from the building anticipation of what we've been imagining daylight will reveal, hoping to collect those perfect images that have been crystallizing in our imaginations for months.

Soon we lose sight of each other.

Steve, whose demeanor is easygoing yet determined, positions himself between two dunes, patiently awaiting first light. He and David met at the University of Maryland in the late '70s while pursuing their doctorates in public communication; he's now a professor at the University of Rhode Island.

Perched atop his personal mountain of sand, Bruce, barely visible to the three others, extends the legs on his tripod in preparation for his first snap. The newest member of the quartet and, irritatingly, the youngest by a couple of years, he's the most outgoing personality among us, quick to smile, offer an opinion, and strike up conversation with strangers. He and David crossed paths in the mid-'70s as fellow communication managers for Marriott Corporation. Bruce headed public relations for the Great America theme park in San Jose, while David served as corporate director of employee communications at company headquarters outside Washington, D.C.

From somewhere in the murky dimness seconds before sunrise, Bruce hears his name called out.

"Bruuuuce, you using the wide angle or big bomba?"

Having just attached his 24mm lens to his Canon camera body, the question prompts him to reconsider his choice. Quickly, he exchanges the stubby wide angle for the long, sleek 400mm telephoto that compresses the faraway and brings it closer. Soon after he purchased that coveted lens, making him the envy of his three compadres, one of the friends referred to it as the "big bomba" (for its physical size and sizable price tag) – and the audacious label stuck. Grinning, he brings his chilled, cupped hands to his mouth and bellows, "The big bomba . . . of course."

For a time, the only sound Bruce picks up is the non-stop "whoosh" of the unstinting desert wind, signaling the ending of night and the coming of day.

Then, just as he's about to repeat himself, the faraway voice reaches him. "Smart ass."

Gratified, he smiles slyly, then mutters something unintelligible under his breath.

· · · · · · · · · · · · · · · · ·

Minutes later, from another dune comes a muffled, yet familiar, voice. "Any place on earth you'd rather be right now, guys?"

Before anyone can react, Steve shouts out fair warning, "Here she comes!"

Two beats later, the first slice of brilliant orange begins tiptoeing across the dunes, waking the sleepy desert. Then, an explosion of light sprays every which way, illuminating the stunning scene in shifting tones of sepia. We're so mesmerized by the natural beauty coming to life before our eyes, we almost forget we have cameras.

But not quite. For the next few seconds, the only sound disturbing the silence enveloping us is the non-stop staccato "click-click-click-click" of camera shutters. Until a very different sound replaces the camera clicks: our voices floating across the now-awakened, sparkling dunes.

"Oh, wow."

"Unbelievable."

"Oh lord, take my camera, my lenses. It can't get any better than this."

"Thank you, Mama Nature."

We are in visual ecstasy, everywhere we look . . . dunes and mountains, shadows and light, curves and lines, dunes and more dunes in every direction, one more magnificent than the next. Then, in what seems no more than the blink of an eye, an extraordinary morning is history, to our chagrin. Exhausted and exhilarated, we climb down from the shimmering dunes, now sizzling with heat, propelled by rubbery legs and gnawing appetites. Though we waited almost a week for the night winds to smooth away the footprint-pocked dunes and had nearly given up hope, finicky Mother Nature eventually rewarded our patience (or heard our prayers?). Our prize for waiting was witnessing an unforgettable dawn in an unforgettable setting, sharing an unforgettable experience, and taking home more than our fair share of unforgettable memories and – hallelujah! – a few unforgettable images.

Slowly, grudgingly, we trek back to the car, deposit our dusty gear in the trunk, and empty our shoes of enough sand to fill several large hourglasses.

As we collapse into the car, at once fulfilled and depleted, not a word is spoken. None needs to be. Each of us knows exactly what the other three are thinking: *This was worth the wait.*

Chapter XXV

....

May 26-27, 2005

....

From: Rick
To: Tom, Dennis, David
Subject: Now, Now, Let's Not Overstate
Date: May 26, 2005

OK. This has been interesting, cathartic, poignant and sad. It's reminded each of us that we're not alone.

I hate to be the party pooper, but I suggest it's time to move on. Let's revel now in the wonders of New Zealand, the amazing accomplishments of children who are forging their own way in the world, the marvels of grandchildren and the love of our families.

Despite the profound tragedy each of us suffered, we are damn lucky.

So, yes, let's take a few minutes to reflect and to be introspective. But let's not wallow in or allow ourselves to be consumed by the tragedy.

Let's raise the proverbial glass (or, better yet, a real one), and toast each other, who we are, and our friendship.

First round is on me!

— Rick

I hate to be the one to disagree with you, Dickie the Party Pooper, after you wrote so eloquently of your past and what it means, but nobody here is wallowing or being consumed. Haven't sensed that at all, really. Quite the opposite, methinks. Am I being defensive?

And I think because of everything that's been said, I believe we all are that much more aware of and grateful for our good fortune, in family and friends, work and life; if this catharsis reminds us of this fact, all the better, I say.

But never being one to refuse frugal Dickie's generous urges, I accept on behalf of my colleagues your offer to buy the first round and toast our fine lives made finer by our increasingly meaningful friendships.

So where and when should we gather to lift our glasses high?

Thank you, Richard J., for being you . . . Shalom, J. David

From: Tommy
To: Rick, Dennis, Davey
Subject: Come to Auckland - and Relax . . .
Date: May 27, 2005

Seems we may all be ready for a timeout. Reliving the heartache and myriad unanswerable questions surrounding our parents' suicides is a form of emotional whiplash we willingly put ourselves through. And while comforting to have this private forum to share what's hidden away inside us, the raw honesty marking these onerous conversations can take its toll on each of us – in ways we may not realize.

And so I propose . . .

We return to Rick's inspired suggestion that we "revel in the wonders of New Zealand." A smashing idea that definitely should be seriously considered, brothers. I can only imagine how the down time together would serve to lighten our emotional load and strengthen our already special bond of friendship.

Remember, each of you and your lovely wives – Karen, Ellen and Mary – have invitations to be our guests anytime in the beautiful Titirangi bush overlooking Auckland. A delightful place for hiking, biking, relaxing, swimming, surfing, relaxing (have I mentioned relaxing?!), etc.

I've gotten spoiled in semi-retirement and just can't keep up this hectic pace!

For now, friends, enjoy the week ahead and savor the pleasure of each new day – and even if that means work. There are times, in the lonely hours half a world away, when I'd jump back into the trenches at VOA in a heartbeat. But the time has come to carve out some new trenches and challenges here in New Zealand.

I'll try to concentrate on moving forward instead of looking back at a place forever changed – but still remembered and missed for all it was.

Take care, mates . . . Tommy

Chapter XXVI

. . . .

August, 2009

. . . .

McCormick & Schmick's, Chicago, IL

· ·

"Who do you guys talk with – besides your wives and us – about your parent's suicide and how it influenced your life?" David asks nobody in particular.

For us, questions like this almost always trigger a sharp "withdraw" reflex. With each other, though, it's different – up to a point.

"No one . . . really," Dennis says. He wants to say more, but changes his mind a few times before adding, reluctantly, "Until David, and then you two, came along."

Tom sips slowly from his near-empty wine glass and scrutinizes the three sets of eyes locked on him, as if he's reading the thoughts hiding behind them.

"I've shared more with you three," he says, "than with anyone else. Ever."

The four of us exchange indiscernible nods. Tom's statement is true for each of us, though to varying extents.

"What about you, Dickson?" David asks, using one of his many nicknames for his long-time friend. "When you want to talk about your mother . . ."

"I don't think about her all that much," Rick jumps in, trying a little too hard to sound indifferent, "except when we're together. At other times, only rarely." Turning toward David, he says in a more mollifying tone, "It's not like the days after we first met, or when we were at the University of Maryland, when . . . when, uh . . ."

David knows what Rick wants to say, and how hard it is to speak the words he's thinking and feeling, so he tries to help. "When we felt a constant need to talk about our mothers, our fathers, our siblings, our family situations. When we felt a need to hear ourselves say what we only thought to ourselves. When we felt a *need* to talk to somebody willing to listen to – and believe – us.

"Thank goodness we had each other, Dickie, or who knows what kind of rascals we would've become."

"Who says you haven't?" Tom asks whimsically. "Become rascals, I mean."

Without missing a beat, he grabs a knife, fork and spoon and shakes them at Rick and David, trying hard but unable to maintain a straight face. "You've always been rascals," he says, eyes twinkling mischievously as a wry grin crinkles his reddish cheeks.

Now, with Dennis privy to the legendary story of the silverware prank, we all share a good laugh.

Bound together by our history, with relationships further deepened during this eyeball-to-eyeball gathering, we toast ourselves, knowing we are friends to the last.

Chapter XXVII

. . . .

June, 1969

. . . .

College Park, MD

. . . .

N o friendship – indeed, no relationship – is without its moments of disagreement. Moments when words fly – rash, hurtful words – that, even when instantly regretted, can't be unsaid. Or unheard.

Yet quarrelling can force to the surface a degree of frankness between comrades that otherwise would remain locked away. Unfiltered openness offers close friends the chance to draw even closer than they were before the argument that temporarily pushed them apart.

"Discord on one level is harmony on another," observed Alan Watts, a noted 20th century British philosopher. In theory, as in life.

. . . .

O ur first joint business venture was the source of our earliest, ugliest and loudest disagreement. Especially for two guys who rarely raise their voices.

During the summer after our sophomore year of college, we both realized we needed more income – for tuition, books, room and board, transportation, nascent social lives – to supplement what we earned from our summer jobs. After exploring our limited options, we took a leap of faith our elders counseled us against ("Are you two nuts, or what?") and launched "Sunday Donuts," a subscription, customized delivery service on Sunday mornings, guaranteed by 8 a.m. or the donuts are on us.

It was demanding work, much tougher and a more time-consuming juggling act than we'd anticipated, and an ongoing mental and logistical challenge as we had to learn how to manage a small business, day by day, problem by problem. Between us, we did everything and anything, from pivotal decisions to trifling details: concept and strategy, marketing and sales, contracting and accounting, and whatever else was needed or required. We negotiated price breaks with a bakery, plotted our fast-expanding delivery route, sorted the customized orders (in the wee hours!), drove the delivery vehicles (our own rickety Ramblers), and collected payments in person.

After sprinkling our target area (a new residential section of Bowie, Maryland) with advance fliers announcing the coming of Sunday Donuts, we followed up with door-to-door, driveway-to-driveway solicitations on weekday evenings and all day on weekends. Our folksy buttonhole pitch seemed to strike a chord with many suburbanites who jumped at the chance to forgo driving to a grocery or donut shop to fetch breakfast, particularly on a leisurely Sunday morning. By Christmas, as word spread, we were juggling deliveries to some 120 homes – *every* Sunday. Both our cars reeked of sugar and dough, but we hardly noticed.

The business took off and increasingly dominated our lives. We did our fair share of complaining about that, but in truth we enjoyed running and building our "baby" into a thriving, mildly profitable enterprise.

The following summer, however, the unremitting pressures and anxieties of the business, on top of those of college, money and anemic social lives (by now, David was engaged to be married to Karen – with Rick, naturally, slated as Best Man), spilled over into our personal relationship.

And, for a few terrible moments, our unshakable friendship was, for the first time, under threat.

. . . .

"You can't leave me high and dry with all this now," David seethes in exasperation, his anger fast-approaching the boiling point. "While you play soldier boy for four damn weeks!"

Not prone to emotional outbursts, Rick is unruffled, his voice modulated. "You're acting as if I just sprang this on you. I told you months ago I'd have to be leaving next month for ROTC camp."

"Get out of it," David demands.

A half-smile, half-scowl creeps onto Rick's face as he confronts David's glare. "I can't. I have a legal obligation and, even if I didn't, I've committed to do this." He hesitates, mulling his next words. "It's important to *me*, and to my future."

The venue for our impromptu shouting match is the main entrance to the stately, six-story McKeldin Library, which faces the grassy mall that is the heart of the sprawling University of Maryland campus.

"Is that so, General Knapp, sir, yes sir." David, face flushed with anger, eyes fixed and unblinking, moves to within inches of Rick, who just stares back, unblinking and unsympathetic. "You, you, you, I get it."

Underlying our outburst this day is not only Rick's ROTC training obligation that will force David to handle their Sunday Donuts route solo, but also our fundamentally differing views on America's involvement in the Vietnam War. Rick doesn't favor war and would support all efforts to avoid it, but his sense of duty to serve when called by the country's leaders left him little choice. David opposes U.S. engagement in Southeast Asia, believing the war is unwinnable and the cost in lives lost exorbitant and immoral. In days prior, we had many edgy debates on the subject, as we each attempted to sway the other to his point of view – without success. Our political and social views, in most instances, have been similar. Vietnam is an exception.

A soaking storm is in full force, adding to the already unbearable humidity typical of Mid-Atlantic summers. David is bathed in perspiration mixed with rain drops; Rick seems somehow to remain bone dry through it all, as usual, a difference between them that is certain to pique David to no end.

With thunder crackling overhead amid bursts of searing light, our hardened gawps of defiance remain stuck in place, as if we were kids again dueling in a stare-down contest. First one to flinch loses. Unless level-headedness somehow intervenes first.

Fortunately, it does. Sort of.

"Do you think I like leaving you short-handed like this?" Rick asks calmly through still-gritted teeth, drawing on his innate compromising nature. The personal slant to the rhetorical question is temporarily disarming, and temperatures begin to cool – but only a degree or two. A frustrated David is annoyed with himself for stupidly spitting out words he already regrets, and annoyed with Rick for his swollen, misplaced sense of righteousness. And, to complete the triad, he's pissed off in general for the lousy predicament he finds himself in.

Shaking his head over and over, he sputters, "Maybe starting this whole damn donuts thing was a giant mistake. Why'd we ever think we could pull this off and not chew each other up in the process? Neither of us is a business major or knows diddly-squat about running a business."

Rick smiles in that knowing way when you realize you've got the perfect rejoinder. "I'd say the evidence – those 120 paying households – strongly suggests otherwise."

Unpersuaded, or not yet willing to enter into a truce, David grumbles, "Guess we'll find out over the next few weeks, won't we?"

Little by little the confrontation loses steam as we revisit points already made to deaf ears, somehow thinking that if we say the same thing enough times it eventually will persuade the other to abandon his position. We finally agree to disagree, an unsatisfying conclusion to an uncomfortable confrontation, and storm off in opposite directions, hurt and perturbed. This is as *unfriendly* as we've ever been.

We don't speak or communicate in any form the entire four weeks Rick is away. The cooling off period lets us regain much of the perspective we lost in the heat of irrational debate.

And fortunately, David's worst fears never materialize.

He and Sunday Donuts survive by relying on the production and distribution process we created together. As planned, we hire David's eager, short-on-cash, future brother-in-law as Rick's stand-in. David makes one substantial change during Rick's absence: the donut sorting venue. Instead of readying the custom orders in the spacious kitchen of Rick's house in Bowie on Saturday nights, the assembly line is crammed into the tiny kitchen in fiancée Karen's parents' house in Takoma Park, a shout away from our donut supplier. Karen, her sisters, and her mom and dad all voluntarily pitch in, somehow convincing themselves that the sorting routine is fun and the overpowering sugary sweet aroma delectable. David pays Karen's brother in cash and the rest of her family members in unsold donuts and profuse thank yous.

Following Rick's return, the air between us stays a bit frosty for a time. Little is said by either of us about our verbal fisticuffs in the pouring rain in front of McKeldin Library; the words and issues at the core of that disagreement remained an unaddressed sore spot until long after we abandoned Sunday Donuts almost a year later.

Inevitably, our friendship, sturdier and more durable than either of us realized, survived that stormy Sunday when we squared off in the only shouting match (to date) of a relationship now spanning more than 50 years . . .

Chapter XXVIII

. . . .

August, 2009

. . . .

McCormick & Schmick's, Chicago, IL

. . . .

For what seems longer than it is, the table is still and silent, as each of us retreats into the comfort, or hell, of his own private memories, many of them awakened from long hibernation during this night of true confessions.

Tables are gradually clearing out for the night, lowering the din of clashing background sounds that fill a restaurant when it's in the whirlwind of prime-time operation.

"It's been 43 years since you and I met on a street corner in Bowie, JD," Rick begins slowly, deliberately. "That was the start of a friendship that has weathered not only time but also thousands of miles. And profound changes in our lives. But we've each been fortunate enough to have other close friends too," – smiling warmly, he nods at Tom and Dennis, in turn – "a number of whom are long-standing and important to us. To who we are."

He stops, stealing a moment to fully consider his point and allow his listeners to do the same, but the expression on Rick's face says he's not done yet. "But no friendship is . . . quite like ours."

David, listening intently, his chin resting in an upturned palm, blinks his agreement.

"But how to put the deeper meaning of our friendship, of any genuine friendship" – Rick glances again at Tom, then Dennis – "into words easily understood and appreciated?"

Though intended as a rhetorical question, Rick can't help himself. "David's been pondering the definition and meaning of friendship for almost as long as I've known him. He's obsessed by it." Rick sneaks a quick side glance at his old friend. "So I've been giving it some thought, too. Even done some research. If for nothing else than to humor David."

In unison, Dennis, Tom and Rick turn to David, who is unfazed by Rick's gentle jab.

"Friendship is so difficult to articulate," Rick persists, his tone and mannerisms taking on the air of a college professor, "it defies definition. Some might use current vernacular to call our relationship a 'bromance,' but that flippant term isn't adequate or accurate in characterizing our relationship. I've heard abstract terms like *harmony*, *accord* and *understanding*, among others, used to explain friendship. All true in our case," he nods, but then switches to shaking his head, adding, "but also insufficient.

"However," he hesitates, thinking further before going on, "maybe insufficient is unavoidable. I don't believe that the true meaning of friendship can be captured in words. Any words. I think Thoreau, or someone from his era, said that."

"Pretty profound," Dennis says. "And definitely true. Much like another term near and dear to each of us, blessed and cursed with endless meanings and interpretations . . . *communication*."

"Hear, hear," David pipes up, a little too enthusiastically, rapping his knuckles on the hardwood table.

"But . . ." says Tom, the retired broadcast journalist never at a loss for words, ". . . but aren't there always words, somewhere, to describe what we mean? Even if we have to hunt for them?"

David wraps both hands around his water glass. "You'd surely think so, Tommy boy, wouldn't you? But I have to wonder. No words I've come across seem to capture the deep down soulful nature of true friendship. None do justice to describing the many aspects – the expectations, responsibilities and behaviors that make up friendships," he points a finger first at himself and then at Tom, Dennis and Rick in turn, "like ours.

"Let's face it. There are friends," David's voice dips low and he uses air quotes to indicate something less, "and there are FRIENDS. These days the term friend is overused and, even worse, misused. Everybody seems to be a friend, whether they really are or not. No thanks to Facebook tagging everyone on its system as a so-called friend, even if they don't know each other from Adam. That cheapens the term, dilutes its meaning and diminishes its impact when the word is used properly."

"But," Dennis notes, playing the contrarian, "isn't it human nature to do that? To refer to people we come in contact with frequently as friends, if just to be polite – rather than labeling them as 'what's his name' or 'the blonde lady down the street?'"

"I'd have to say yes, it is," Tom says with conviction, filling his spoon with a dollop of cheesecake and holding it at the ready. "I probably refer to lots of folks as friends who aren't. Not strictly speaking. Not nearly a friend in the same way any of you are."

The spoon finds Tom's mouth, and he's in heaven again.

"Can't disagree," David admits, shrugging. "That's reality. We all do it. But Rick's right. I've been pondering the notion of friendship for decades. And, as Alice in Wonderland said, it just gets *curiouser* and *curiouser* the deeper I dig."

"How so?" says Dennis, leaning in.

David rocks forward onto his elbows and interlocks his fingers, thumbs pointing skyward. "The simple truth I've discovered is . . . not all friendships are created equal. Every friendship is unique, a one-of-a-kind relationship. Like snowflakes. One is never identical to another. Every friendship is a distinct mix of intersecting interests, histories, behaviors, vocabulary, customs and habits, activities, expectations, and on and on it goes. I believe we know in our hearts who is a friend in the true *meaning* of the term. That's irrespective of the popular street language or synonyms found in *Roget's Thesaurus*, yet the common language we use, and rely on, is important, sometimes critically so. Because if we don't differentiate our few genuine friends from the countless other acquaintances we're merely *friendly with*, we risk blurring the actual distinction between them. And when that happens, soon every so-called friend becomes pretty much like every other one."

"Why do we all tend to do that?" Dennis wonders aloud.

The four of us share pensive stares once again.

Chapter XXIX

....

October, 2004

....

Prague, Czech Republic

· ·

Who among us has been spared the heartbreak – and trauma – of living through at least one catastrophic loss that shook our faith in humanity and recast our future?

How did we initially react – and ultimately respond? Did we close our eyes tight or open them wide? Were we able to look far enough beyond the tragedy, the angst, the ambiguity to stop seeing ourselves as victims and move on with life?

"We cannot have a world where everyone is a victim," writes scholar and social critic Camille Paglia. "'I'm this way because my father made me this way. I'm this way because my husband made me this way.' Yes, we are indeed formed by traumas that happen to us. But then you must take charge, you must take over, you are responsible."

· · · · · · · · · · · · · · · · ·

After Ellen and Rick married, she met David and Karen for the first time in New York City in 1987, when the four of us began planning our first vacation together: a week in what turned out to be wet, yet wonderful London the following year. It would be the first of many domestic and international excursions together over the next 30 years. Among those treasured trips, history-rich Prague stands out in our recollections – for all it was, all it is, and all it did to remind us that, in a universal sense, *we are who we were.*

It is a magnificently designed, picturesque city with a checkered past where any number of languages and dialects can be heard at any moment. Prague's castle on the hill and the Charles Bridge over the Vltava River are exquisite testaments to the vision, craftsmanship and artistry of those who conceived and built these timeless structures centuries ago. Some historians argue it was Prague's beauty and charm that so captured Adolf Hitler's imagination that he spared the city from Germany's brutal bombing campaigns.

Most mornings, before Karen and Ellen are ready to experience the city, the two of us walk to the grand, statue-lined bridge, cameras in hand and eyes wide open to photographic possibilities. We are inspired and eager despite the omnipresent chill and mist. Only one of us is, however, a natural early riser. So, each morning around 6, David phones Rick and asks, "Coming?" A groggy Rick croaks "yep" or "nope" and David then proceeds solo or waits for his buddy. Of course, David still takes great delight in reminding Rick in no uncertain terms that the most exquisite sunrise of the week happened on a "nope" morning.

During these unhurried morning photo shoots, several hours before Prague's streets and bridges are stuffed with locals and tourists, we typically start out together, then drift off in separate directions, enticed by some pattern or reflection or grouping of elements. Also typically, we soon reconnect and share our favorite shots, offering each other feedback on composition or lighting or exposure. After that, more often than not, we'd team up and reshoot some of those same images, building on suggestions for improving them, by finding a better angle or integrating an aspect of the scene that one of us missed.

· · · · · · · · · · · · · · · · ·

One day we hire a local guide – Pavel, a rabbinical student and native of the city – to take Ellen and the two of us through the centuries-old Jewish Quarter. Karen is working and misses the tour.

Pavel explains that this decrepit Jewish section, like the rest of Prague, has its own haunting beauty, decaying majesty and tragic history. All three of us are captivated, but for the two of us, as Jews only a generation removed from the atrocities of the Holocaust, being here carries deeper meaning than it would otherwise.

The Old Jewish Cemetery, a few blocks from the river, is packed with nameless, moss-covered tombstones leaning every which way. Some are worn smooth by time. Others have been defaced. Many are falling apart. Pavel explains that graves are stacked as many as 12 deep, since the space allotted for the one Jewish cemetery was constrained on all sides by overcrowded tenements to which Jews were confined for centuries.

• • • • • • • • • • • • • • • •

A djacent to the cemetery is the Pinkas Synagogue, originally built in the early 16th century and the second oldest surviving synagogue in Prague.

We find ourselves alone, standing shoulder to shoulder, taking in the austere structure that looks more like a big family house than a place of worship. A small Star of David on the façade, painted the same dull brown as the rest of the building, is all that identifies the building as a synagogue.

"Look," Rick points at a street marker with the synagogue's name. "They misspelled your name. All these years, and you never told me you owned a synagogue."

Repressing a grin, David is intrigued by the idea.

The irony of the comment is not lost on either of us. It has been a decade or so since we attended Yom Kippur services together in Cleveland. Although we both feel a strong connection to our Jewish heritage and the moral values inherent in its teachings, neither of us is an observant Jew.

"The closest I've ever come to feeling like I owned a synagogue," David says, peering off into the distance, retreating half a century in his memory, "is right after my mother died. When I practically lived in one. Orthodox, no less. My grandfather pushed me – gently, as was his way – to go before school to say *Kaddish* for my mother's memory. He handed me his *tallis* [prayer shawl] and *siddur* [prayer book] to use, his subtle way of insisting I go and be a good Jewish son. And so I did, because it was him, who I loved and respected as much as anybody. And, I guess, because I was still reeling from the shock of her unnatural death, a lost boy who hadn't yet figured out anything for myself.

"That synagogue – strongly East European – was much like this one except smaller. Could fit two or three of those into this one. It was squeezed between a dry cleaners and a bakery, easy to miss if you didn't know it was there. Right along Coney Island Avenue, just a few blocks from my aunt and uncle's place. My dad, sister and I lived with them for a short while after my mother's burial."

"You've never told me this," Rick says, a bit surprised.

"Really?" David seems to be only half listening. "You sure about that? I must've."

Rick shakes his head, but lets it go. "So, how often did you go? Every Sabbath?"

"Every day. Even on weekends. The 7 a.m. sunrise service. Just me and maybe 20 of the most devout worshipers. All in beards and side curls, dressed in nothing but black. And most my grandfather's age – or older."

"Bet you blended right in." Rick tries to suppress a grin, unsuccessfully.

But David doesn't react; he has retreated to another time and place. "During services, I'd sit by myself, stand up to recite *Kaddish*, and then leave as soon as it was over. I didn't know anybody. Only a few spoke any English. But after a while, I came to tolerate, maybe even look forward to, being there. For the solitude, and being by myself. Thinking my own thoughts . . . without somebody else telling me how I *ought* to think and how I *should* feel about things only I could feel."

"Listening to you," Rick says, "reminds me of the months after my mother died, when my sister and I would sit in silence in our temple's sanctuary before Sunday school, just the two of us, in the dark. Except for the red glow of the Eternal Light."

"Why did you do that?"

"Good question. I don't really remember. Guess we needed some quiet time. It felt good being there, just the two of us; having the place to ourselves. It was peaceful, safe. The solitude allowed us to think, to contemplate. I recall looking at the Eternal Light, a symbol of hope. It was the only light in the darkened sanctuary."

"Did you feel . . ." – David hesitates – ". . . closer to . . . your mom?"

"Never thought about that before now, but I probably did or . . . I must have . . ." Now it's Rick whose eyes get that glassy, faraway look for several moments.

Returning to David's synagogue story, Rick asks, "So why did your grandfather push you to go to services every day?"

"I never asked, and Gramps never volunteered," David admits. "But he grew up in a kosher home where practicing strict Judaism rituals was a way of life, a life he never completely abandoned. So to him, it was the natural thing to do. More than that, though, I think he believed it was the right thing to do. He told me so when I balked, reluctant to even try it . . . by myself. I guess he believed it would somehow help me sort things out. Perhaps come to terms, to whatever extent I could, with my mother's terrible choice. Just how that was supposed to happen by sitting through services in a language I barely understood, we never talked about."

"And did it?"

"Not at first, certainly, when I was a robot just going through the motions, not knowing why. Maybe I did it so my grandfather would think me a good person . . . like he was. Or maybe I wanted to do something meaningful for my poor mother. But – and I can't really explain it – the longer I went, the less I resisted and the more I got out of it. Even so, after about seven months, I knew I'd said *Kaddish* enough. I didn't tell anyone when I stopped going. Not even Gramps. He never said a word to me, though I'm sure my aunt told him I'd given it up. I think he must've known there was no predicting how long I'd need the daily soul-searching routine of praying, thinking, remembering, escaping."

"When you stopped going, did you feel you were letting him down?" Rick asks. "Or yourself?"

"Hmmm, tough question. Never really thought about that." David smiles to himself as he considers the question. "Did I let myself down? Don't think so. And Gramps? Maybe. Or maybe not. He was a 'live and let live' type who accepted people for who they were, and didn't think any less of them because they weren't like him or who he thought they should be. If I could ask him today what he wanted me to gain from muttering the *Kaddish* in front of unsmiling strangers every morning, I suspect he'd say something like, 'Anything good to be found there was for you to discover. But you never would if you didn't go – and try.'"

"Wise man, your grandfather."

"That he was . . . in his own quiet way." Pausing, David waits for the lump in his throat to pass. "For me," he croaks in a strained whisper, "it was the right thing to do. For several reasons. Gramps just seemed to know intuitively it would be, but only if I found it within myself . . . for myself.

"I'm not sure how or why, but 55 years later, I can still recite the *Kaddish* from memory. It plays in my head like a phonograph record that never stops turning . . . *Yis'ga'dal, vi'yis'ka'dash sh'ma'rabbo . . .*"

"I have no doubt your grandfather hears you," Rick mutters, just loud enough to be heard over David's garbled Hebrew chanting.

David smiles warmly at the pleasing thought that his grandfather might be listening to his soft chanting of the *Kaddish* now, much as he did every morning for a short time during the tumult of late 1961 . . . "*b'olmo de'vroo chir'u'say . . .*"

· · · · · · · · · · · · · · · · ·

By this time, Ellen and Pavel are signaling for us to join them as they enter the old, worn Pinkas Synagogue – a synagogue that, like Prague itself, has defied time and myriad threats.

In an alcove inside the synagogue, we stand together in awed silence studying the plain stucco walls stenciled with more than 77,000 names of those murdered by the Nazis, organized by town and by family. Multiple generations were wiped out. Close by, bringing those names to life, are haunting drawings by doomed Jewish children, each with the child's name scrawled in his or her own hand, all created at the encouragement of a teacher who knew they would never experience adulthood, their fates already sealed.

Like so many other inhumane and inexplicable things in life, we can only lament . . . and wonder why.

Chapter XXX

....

August, 2009

....

McCormick & Schmick's, Chicago, IL

• •

Almost an hour has passed since the dessert menus were delivered and orders placed. It is well after 10 now, and the restaurant has thinned out considerably. Aside from us, only four or five other tables are still active, downing their last sweet bites and lingering over after-dinner liqueurs.

The earlier background buzz – a cacophony of competing conversations, piped-in background music, and the jangles of dishes and silverware – has dwindled to a muted muffle bordering on eerie. We can hear one another speaking at normal volume, if not a notch or two below.

Tom is the only one still dawdling over his dessert. No, make that David's unfinished dessert: a half-eaten, plump wedge of overly creamy pineapple cheesecake. Never one to let good food go to waste, regardless of whose plate it happens to be on, Tom is always ready to lend a helping hand. In contrast to Rick, who's known for gobbling his food as if somebody's about to grab it, Tom savors every bite with a robust lip smack followed by a moan of delight as he chews in luxurious slow-motion.

The evening is winding down, but none of us is yet willing to declare it over. So we linger purposely, and purposefully, any way we can.

As Tom lifts the last crumbs of cheesecake to his mouth, David's voice pulls him from his gastronomic reverie. "Tommy, you talked of missing your dad's presence in your life. But how do you make peace with the heartache he caused you by choosing suicide over life? As we each know, that's an ache that never stops gnawing at your conscience."

The question seems to visibly dim Tom's mood, but he doesn't let it derail him. "Over the years, I've come to rely on a strategy for coping that's worked for me. It's simple, really. I look at each day as precious, as special. And I try to live each one to the fullest, getting the maximum satisfaction from it. Helps me to minimize time spent second-guessing myself as to what I could've done to make Dad, and me, happier." He lets out a lengthy sigh, a mix of melancholy and gratification. "I feel blessed and happy . . . with Jenny, my family and my many good friends around the USA and New Zealand."

"You make it sound awfully easy leapfrogging from being wracked with guilt for decades to suddenly feeling blessed and grateful for each day," Dennis says, his innate cynicism and curiosity surfacing simultaneously. "How is that possible? How do you make that psychological leap every morning?"

"I get it, Denny, I think," David jumps in, pushing aside his empty dessert plate to make room for his elbows. "After I awoke from bypass surgery, having accepted that I might not, suddenly everything – and everybody – looked different to me. Brighter, nicer, kinder . . . in all ways, better than before. But I soon realized the only thing that had changed was . . ." – his voice catches, fighting off his mounting emotions – "was *me*. How I saw others, and myself. Just like that, I was more tolerant, more patient, more forgiving, more present in *every* moment. For about a year, that's who I'd become. So I thought. But then those feelings, that way of seeing and being, began to fade . . ." David sniffles back tears. "It's still part of me," he says in a tone lined with regret, "but it's part of the background now. You'd think it a simple matter to summon back. Not so, unfortunately. Some things, most often those we cherish or desire most, look easier to do than they really are."

"Looks can be deceiving," Tom says, unperturbed by Dennis' doubts and bolstered by David's self-reflections, his eyes riveted on the snifter of golden-brown amaretto in front of him. "In my case, the perspective shift wasn't easy and didn't happen quickly, I can tell you that. In fact, it took years, most of a lifetime, to reach this shaky accommodation with myself. How did I get here? Not sure if it's one thing or another, if truth be told. Age. Time. Need, maybe . . . " He grinds to a stop, needing a drink. First, he inhales the liqueur's sweet almond aroma, then lifts the shiny cordial glass toward his mouth, but before it gets there he becomes distracted by another thought. "Or maybe it was as basic as confronting my own mortality and realizing I wanted more than anything to live another day, another month, another year, another decade, feeling good about myself . . . and my life."

Sitting back with a soft thump, a look of wary wonder filling his eyes, Dennis mutters under his breath, "Incredible . . . if only I could."

Tom gazes pensively into the translucent liquid before taking a tiny sip, holding it on his tongue as a prelude to swallowing – and, of course, relishing it thoroughly.

More thoughts are coming to him now in rapid succession, propelling him forward. "With that sobering realization came, I think, a pent up need to let go of dark, unhealthy feelings I'd held onto for too long. Jagged feelings that were starting to eat me up inside. Betrayal, frustration, guilt, emptiness, to note a few. What good was I deriving from holding in all these combustible emotions until they explode and destroy me, as happened to my father . . . ?" – he takes in, one after another, the three rapt faces fixed on his – ". . . and to your mothers?"

· · · · · · · · · · · · · · · · ·

For a time, nobody moves a muscle as the harsh, bittersweet reality of Tommy's confession registers with the three other sons and merges with their own memories of their lost parents.

Of course, each had considered similar thoughts thousands of times before, but maybe never quite in these terms and certainly not in a setting such as this, surrounded by kindred spirits who understand as few others do the deeper implications of a loved one's death by suicide.

"Perhaps," Tom says, his deep, buttery voice puncturing the quiet, "and I've not thought this before this very moment, it was an inner alarm going off, warning me to not let go of my reflex for self-preservation, my deep-down desire to live . . . as a way of counteracting my father's desire to die."

"Wow, that was heavyweight stuff, Thomas, stated crisply and succinctly," Dennis says.

Tom rolls his eyes.

"You know," Tom says, "I didn't expect that talking face-to-face about our parents' suicides would be any different than our email exchange of a few years ago. But I was wrong. Sitting here, all of us together, eye-to-eye, reaction-to-reaction, is an entirely different experience. Spoken words, well, they carry more weight, more meaning, more realism. You're able to not only sense but see the emotions while hearing the words, rather than having to try imagining them while reading the words on a computer screen, sitting all by yourself."

"You're right, Tom," says Dennis. "Writing – or reading – words on a page, though powerful in its own way, triggers different senses than, say, tonight's impromptu discussion . . . seeing your faces, observing your shifting expressions and gestures, hearing the tone of your voices expressing your instantaneous reactions."

"Who else do you talk to like *this*?" Rick asks.

"Almost nobody," Tom says. "With you guys, I'm comfortable talking about any and all aspects of what I went through during the most difficult time in my life. I'm eternally grateful that, at various points in time, we've been there for each other. I feel a special kinship with each of you, built up over the years since the four of us began talking and writing about the, uh, tragic events in our lives we unfortunately have in common." Pausing for a breath or for effect, or maybe both, Tom lifts the shapely liqueur glass to his mouth with an understated flourish. "The highest compliment I can pay each of you is to express to you . . . individually . . . and collectively . . . just how much . . . I cherish our friendship."

"Hear, hear," David pronounces for a second time this evening, banging the table. This time he draws inquisitive stares from the few diners still lingering in a now-hushed McCormick & Schmick's. Dennis and Rick add supportive, but softer, knocks.

Virtually unnoticed, our waiter deftly places the leatherette check folder at the center of the table, then fades away.

"Since we're talking friendship," Dennis says, "I've come to value it now even more than I did earlier in life. Maybe it's my age. But I know now how valuable social connections are to one's health, even more so as we get older and are less likely to have outside connections, but that's a side benefit to the pleasure I get out of human contact.

"Learning about each of your experiences with suicide has made me more aware that suicide is not as rare as I once thought – and that makes it a less bizarre part of my history. While I don't begin conversations with friends or acquaintances with, 'Hi, my mom committed suicide,' I'm no longer reticent to mention it, if it seems appropriate. Meaning, I suppose, I'm not nearly as embarrassed about, or afraid to bring up, the subject of suicide . . . as I once was."

The other three sons nod in agreement.

Toward the end of our intensive 4-way email exchange four years earlier, we all admitted to feeling mentally and emotionally exhausted; we needed to let go of the unresolved past and return to the still-unfolding present. Though nobody says as much now, we've reached that fatigue threshold again. It's time to stop. Until next time . . .

For the longest time, we sit quietly, wistfully, content just being in each other's presence.

. . . .

Lights in the restaurant start flickering in a not-so-subtle hint that the Cinderella hour has arrived.

"Time to pay the piper," Tom says. And then, as if cued remotely by an off-stage director, we all reach for the check at once, trading dubious stares. Then, just as quickly, we all pull back our hands as if they'd been slapped, and share a good laugh, at ourselves and each other.

"Be my guest, JD," Rick says to David, gesturing loftily with an open palm.

"Wouldn't want to insult you, Dickie. After you . . . *please*." Mimicking Rick's exaggerated hand flourish with one of his own, David's mild taunt propels us into one of our customary routines.

"You know what my uncle would say, don't you?" David says, eyes twinkling. He peers at Rick, who plays along without missing a beat, fighting back the grin niggling at the corners of his mouth.

"It's better to owe than nah . . ."

David snaps up a hand to stop him. ". . . than not to pay," he finishes the axiom we've been reciting incessantly since our high school days.

And, of course, it isn't the first time Tom or Dennis has endured our *faux* Laurel and Hardy routine. But considering the occasion and the late hour, our timing is impeccable and, knowing that, we trade lighthearted laughs.

In hindsight, ending this mostly serious dinner discussion on a frivolous note seems fitting. After all, at that moment, who knew when, or if, we would get another chance to sit together and pour out our hearts and souls.

. . . .

The rest of the weekend goes as planned. Baseball, pizza, the architectural boat tour, a farewell dinner at a highly recommended Asian restaurant a few blocks from our hotel. We don't talk of suicide or our deceased parents, only of our lives in the here and now. And of our extraordinary coming together and the undeniable sense of brotherhood we feel and take with us for safekeeping.

From our gathering in Chicago, David heads to New York City to visit family. While en route, up among the clouds, he drafts an email he will send to his fellow sons of suicide:

I keep thinking of our time together and its sweet perfection. The place, the people, the weather, the timing, the conversations (collective and one-on-one), the food, the walking, the sharing, the boat ride, the remembering . . . all part of the first meeting of our private little club.

Tommy, thanks for coming the farthest and providing the excuse for the get together in a neutral city – and for reminding us that true friendship is not affected by distance.

Denny, thanks for coming early and sharing that time with me (I loved our walk/talk) – and for reminding us that true friendship knows no time or age boundaries; it happens when it's supposed to.

Dickie, thanks for, well, being you and always there for me no matter what – and for reminding me to never forget how fortunate I am to have all that I have in my life, despite early setbacks, and for reminding all of us that true friendship is forever.

. . . .

Today, we four are closer than most friends could ever hope to be.

In truth, the depth of our crisscrossing relationships and the potency of the bonds that bind us aren't reflected in the frequency of either our communication (it's sporadic, but thank goodness for email) or face-to-face powwows. (The inaugural gathering in Chicago remains, as of this writing, the one and only time we've all been together).

Proof, perhaps, as Thoreau suggested, that real friendship is much more about *meanings* than words.

Chapter XXXI

....

Late 1971

....

Pease AFB, NH

. . . .

Rick answers the beige wall phone in the kitchen of the small on-base townhouse.

He is on his first active-duty assignment – a green second lieutenant and public information officer at Pease Air Force Base on the New Hampshire seacoast.

"It happens," the hushed yet bubbly voice on the other end of the line says with no introduction.

None is needed, nor is an interpretation of the two-word declaration. It's David, telling his best friend that he and Karen are, as he would later boast, "with child."

Seven months later, Jeffrey Brian is born. And Rick, of course, is named his godfather.

Epilogue

....

May 8-10, 2017

....

From: **Rick**
To: David
Subject: ***Unexpected Dinner Companions***
Date: May 8, 2017

JD –

This is unbelievable.

Last night, Ellen and I were at a casual party with three other couples. Before dinner, the four of us guys were sipping cocktails and one of them asked what I've been doing since I retired. I ran through a list: volunteer work, some travel and family events, and the book we're writing. One of the guys asked what the book was about. I briefly described it, and one of the men – I'd met him before but don't know him well – volunteered that his father had committed suicide when he was 19.

An amazing coincidence, yet again! I was taken aback. Stunned. With the other two looking on, we briefly discussed the profound mental and emotional toll a loved one's suicide can take on those closest to them and, in particular, the long-term effects on the children left behind. For the most part in this brief exchange, I was relating the kinds of issues we deal with in our book, an almost detached and very brief summary of what we've been writing.

It was an informal gathering of friends, and so the dark subject of suicide seemed inappropriate, but as we finished this short exchange our host opined that our book would likely prompt others like us to "come out of the woodwork" with their suicide stories. I didn't think twice about his comment at the time, and the conversation shifted to more upbeat, familiar subjects: Go Cavs! Go Indians!

A couple of hours later, after a wonderful dinner and great conversation, I found myself alone for a moment with our host (the other couples had already left). And *he* confided in me that *his* mother had killed herself when he was 18. I was floored, yet again. Clearly, he didn't feel comfortable revealing that in front of the others, and he said he talks to nobody about this (sound familiar?). Even his adult daughter doesn't know that her grandmother took her own life.

And now I better understood his earlier comment about others coming out of the woodwork.

So maybe our "chance" meeting in Bowie more than 50 years ago and the discovery that Dennis and Tom each lost a parent to suicide may not be quite as uncommon as we thought. I read recently that every person who takes her own life leaves behind 135 or so survivors whose lives are changed in some way forever. In that same article, I was stunned to learn that suicide is among the 10 leading causes of death in the U.S.; nearly 45,000 people chose to kill themselves last year, and that number is growing.

So, it seems, there are more than a few of us survivors around.

It also strikes me that our host's reluctance to talk about his mother's suicide is so typical of children of suicide, particularly among our generation. Maybe there's a bit more acceptance and awareness of aspects of suicide now, but there certainly was a stigma associated with it when we went through the heartbreaking deaths of our mothers.

We'll talk more later.

— Rick

From: David
To: Rick
Subject: Mind Boggling, Indeed
Date: May 9, 2017

Dickie —

History, it appears, continues to repeat itself. Seems unimaginable, doesn't it?

Three of four men, all Baby Boomers and casual friends, reveal that, as teenagers, they were each scarred by the suicide of a parent. Haven't we heard that unlikely story a few times before?

Your account of the dinner party was rattling around in my brain while at the gym this morning, pedaling away on the stationary bike – going nowhere fast – with my thoughts drifting every which way. And suddenly I was catapulted back to that extraordinary evening at McCormick & Schmick's in Chicago when Tommy, Dennis, you and I came together face-to-face for the first time. We'd shared our stories via email a few years before, but this was different. Eyeball-to-eyeball, heart-to-heart, we held nothing back.

Our discussion that night is still piercingly vivid in my mind. Our conversation then, as I recall, was reflective, sobering, but not at all morbid. Sure, there were moments of sadness, frustration and speculation of what might've been, but they were accompanied by recollections of happier times before and after the suicides.

I'll always remember – and try never to take for granted – the overwhelming sense of belonging and pure friendship I felt during that dinner in Chicago.

Precious few survivors of suicide, I imagine, ever find others like themselves, who lived through the nightmare and are willing to discuss openly the gritty details of a disheartening experience they'd give almost anything to wipe from their memories. We're the lucky exception, I expect. Which is why your host's reaction a couple of nights ago – namely his reluctance to share with anyone that his mother had ended her life – doesn't surprise me. Sometimes, it's an inner struggle just to say the word suicide.   It's a sinister word, a horrific act. Whenever I hear it spoken or see it written, it slaps me hard across the face, a jarring reminder of the void created in my life by my mother's decision to end her life prematurely. And even tougher than hearing somebody else utter the word is hearing it come out of my own mouth. It sticks in my throat and gags me even now, over half a century later, an oversized cotton ball impossible to swallow or spit out.

I believe you're right about the stigma associated with suicide having lessened over time, though it certainly hasn't disappeared. I'm thinking about how your Dad twisted the newspaper reporter's arm not to use the word suicide in your mother's obituary. For us, there was guilt, shame, embarrassment and confusion – not to mention the haunting, impossible-to-resolve questions. Others looked at us, the kids left behind in the wake of a parent's suicide, with pity or scorn, even apprehension, as if through guilt by genetic association we were somehow a danger to ourselves, or others. There was much less known about suicide and its causes then. Some seemed to think something must be mentally wrong with *us*, given that our mothers chose to kill themselves, or that we somehow contributed to the insanity that led them to make the awful final decision of their lives. I even sensed that a few people felt my mother's suicide doomed me to a similar fate. I can't deny wondering many of those same things myself for a lot of years.

While there's no question that survivors of suicide today still experience many of the same self-destructive emotions and face many of the same reactions from others, it is no longer the taboo subject it was for generations. There's much more public awareness and discussion of suicide. We know of too many celebrities who killed themselves, many of them revered, talented, brilliant, wealthy, seemingly with everything to live for. Robin Williams and Marilyn Monroe come to mind.

And help today for the person contemplating suicide and survivors like us is much more readily available than it was when our mothers – and we – *needed* it. Increasingly, suicide is viewed as a mental health issue, rooted in depression, rather than dismissed as merely a human weakness or frailty. There are suicide prevention hotlines, trained counselors, support groups, nonprofit associations. And the media have spotlighted the suicide phenomenon and all it entails, nudging it further out of the shadows.

Still, in spite of this growing transparency, one thing remains unchanged: the pain of a loved one's decision to take her or his own life is an indescribable hell for those left behind.

Remember that *Sports Illustrated* article I sent you about Ryan Anderson, the pro basketball player whose fiancée took her life? For a while he was so devastated he couldn't function, and had to take a leave of absence from his team. It took him well over a year to start reconciling his clashing feelings and begin to overcome his paralyzing grief.

When a popular, national magazine like *Sports Illustrated* devotes resources to an in-depth feature discussing the emotional issues encountered by an athlete-survivor of a loved one's suicide, it says something meaningful about society's shifting perceptions of, and desire to better understand, suicide, and, as the Ryan Anderson case exemplifies (not to mention the four sons of suicide's examples), its shattering impact on the lives of their closest loved ones left behind.

Peace, my friend.

— David

P.S. Been to an Indians game lately? No better way to clear the mind – and memory.

From: **Rick**
To: David
Subject: *Reflections on Chicago*
Date: May 9, 2017

Yes, I remember that article about Anderson. It was moving and rang all too true.

And you correctly pointed out that many more helping resources are available today than when we were teenagers trying to make sense of our mothers' suicides. Back then, I don't know that there were psychiatrists, psychologists or other counselors specializing in helping children of suicide. But there couldn't have been many, and they couldn't rely on the considerable body of research on suicide that's been generated in the last 50-plus years.

Add to that the fact that we were kids, reliant on guidance from our fathers who would hardly admit what happened, let alone reach out for help for themselves or their children.

For me, then, nothing could compare to the way close friendships have eased the pain, emptiness, and uncertainties we carry with us always. You and I are proof of that, as is our friendship with Tom and Dennis, ever reminding us of the role we've played in helping one another find some degree of solace, of understanding, of acceptance.

All of those emotions and doubts surfaced that night in McCormick & Schmick's almost a decade ago. We shared disquieting memories of our parents and pondered how the arc of our lives was reshaped in the wake of their deaths.

Thinking back, I am still impressed – and touched – by the naked honesty of our difficult revelations in what amounted to a group soul session, a fitting term since we bared our souls to each other and forged unbreakable bonds. Throughout the evening, there was a palpable sensation of understanding, genuine warmth and empathy. Without hesitating, we each shared our most intimate feelings and recollections, and responded to unnerving queries with disarming candor, sometimes haltingly, more often eloquently. Everything felt right, and safe.

We learned and reconfirmed a great deal that evening. We know, for example, that the unanswerable *why* questions will remain unanswered. That void can never be filled. Our hearts will continue to ache.

Yet, looking back on the 50-plus years since we lost our mothers, I would say we are two, and now four, lucky guys. Our dinner in Chicago affirmed that we are not alone. And that recent dinner gathering I mentioned reaffirmed it.

Bottom-line? We got thrown a tough break early in life, maybe as tough as they come. But our lives have been about much more than that. We are blessed with close friends and supportive spouses and extended families. We have led fulfilling lives – with much more to come.

— Rick

P.S. Got two tix for Sunday's Indians/Twins game. Join me?

From: **David**
To: Rick
Subject: *Group Send-Off*
Date: May 10, 2017

Where did you say your seats are for the Indians game, Dickie? Oh, how I'd love to. Dogs and peanuts, my treat; drinks, we'll negotiate.

A final thought – a P.S. if you will – on our dinner in Chicago.

On the morning of our final day, I was given a send-off by the three of you that captured in the simplest of human gestures the very essence of the group friendship we enhanced and solidified during our weekend together.

"We had said our good-byes the night before," I wrote in my journal, "so I was touched that all three guys rose earlier than they needed to in order to join me for a hurried 15-minute breakfast. I had the earliest flight by far, and hadn't expected to see them again. Then, of course, after I did, I didn't want to leave."

Some bonds cut deep into one's soul and pass close enough to the heart that they become permanent, unbreakable, impervious to the effects of time and geography.

Some bonds persist no matter what. Some bonds just are.

If anyone understands that, Rick, it's us.

"When we can talk about our feelings,
they become less overwhelming,
less upsetting, and less scary.
The people we trust with that important talk
can help us know that we are not alone."

— Fred Rogers

Acknowledgments

From the moment we conceived *Sons of Suicide* to the moment the manuscript became a book, some six years went by. We had estimated it would take two, maybe three. We needed lots of help along the way; fortunately, we got it.

We owe many people our deep thanks for helping us as we created, refined and worked to publish *Sons of Suicide*.

A big debt of gratitude to our wives, Ellen Mattingly and Karen Pincus, for their patience, unflinching honesty, encouragement and timely kicks to our butts to get on with the project. They were – and are – our biggest fans and severest critics. Their insights and suggestions as they read several versions of the manuscript helped shape this book and made it better. And it was the two of them who convinced us that our story could help others get through the ordeal of traumatic loss. So we abandoned our original intent to print a few copies just for family and close friends. Thank you. We each love you both.

Our daughters, Shelby Mattingly and Megan Pincus Kajitani, both avid readers and writers, also were kind enough to read our early manuscript and revisions. Their input and counsel were invaluable in shaping the story's complex structure and sensitive subject matter. And they each cheered us on when we most needed it.

Jeffrey Pincus, David's son, designed the book cover and website. He was able to take sometimes ambiguous direction and turn it into something tangible and meaningful – always with enthusiasm and a wonderful sense of humor.

And Evelyn Peelle lent her expertise to create the look of the book, putting up with our last minute changes, incessant questions and suggestions – all without complaint.

Our Foto Friends, Bruce Burtch and Steve Wood, put up with our jabbering about this project and peppering them with questions while the four of us were on photo trips and at various other points, yet they still were kind enough to review the manuscript and offered valuable suggestions. They also gave us the benefit of their experience and expertise as we crafted and thought through various issues related to publishing and distributing *Sons of Suicide*. Their friendship is an important part of this book and of our lives.

Our friend, Kathy Hogg, generously devoted many hours to editing and proofing our manuscripts. With her keen and precise eye, she not only caught typos and grammatical errors, but also flagged narrative that was unclear or could be improved. She did a phenomenal job on both counts.

Many other family members, friends, former colleagues, and acquaintances shared their thoughts about and reactions to our project. Some helped as we considered how to approach the publishing process, others suggested ways we could ensure our book would reach those who it could most help, and many read various drafts of the manuscript and gave us insightful feedback. Included on this list are people we did not know – clinicians, other survivors of suicide loss, and those who experienced other types of traumatic loss.

Our most sincere thanks go to Paul Azoulay, Susan Azoulay, Mark Bacon, Kyla Braun, Julie Cerel, Ph.D., Karsha Chang, Jeff Chokel, Joanna Connors, Andy Core, Ann Meyers Drysdale, Jane Dystel, Lance Foster, M.D., Arthur Friedman, Nancy Friedman, John Godt, Tom Harrison, Tyler Hicks-Wright, Kathleen Hall Jamieson, Ph.D., Rev. Dr. Beth Johnson, Alex Kajitani, Nicole Kent, Ph.D., Dave Kieffer, Elizabeth Knapp, Michael Knapp, Bob LaGuardia, Ph.D., Terri Luria, Jenny Mahoney, Vanessa McGann, Ph.D., Mike Meliker, Gretchen Miller, Jessica Miller-Stern, John O'Leary, Anne O'Leary-Kelly, Ph.D., Rick Oliver, Laura Orkin, Rosemarie Owens, Michael Palgon, Regina Phelps, Harold Rudnick, Jim Salmon, M.D., Bill Shumard, Betty Vandermause, Brig. Gen. Tim White, Ph.D., and Danno Wolkoff.

And, of course, huge notes of thanks go to our close friends and fellow "sons," Tom Mahoney and "Dennis." They were generous in allowing us to use the intimate emails they wrote long before this project was conceived, then opened up further by answering questions that fleshed out their stories. Their candor and willingness to bare their souls and open their hearts are central to the story of *Sons of Suicide*.

About the Authors

Rick Knapp (right in the photo) and David Pincus have been close friends since meeting as high school seniors more than 50 years ago. Both attended the University of Maryland as undergraduates – Rick in journalism and David in political science. Subsequently, Rick earned his M.A. in journalism at The Ohio State University, while David stayed at Maryland for his Master's and Ph.D. in organizational communication.

Following stints in the U.S. Air Force and at AT&T, Rick's professional life was spent as a management consultant, partner and leader with global consulting firms Foster Higgins and Mercer, focusing on employee and organizational communication, and human resources. He retired in 2012, but has yet to slow down. He serves on the boards of Cleveland Play House, America's first regional theatre, and ideastream, the public media organization in Northeast Ohio. Among his passions are photography, cooking, baseball and travel. He and his wife Ellen live in Cleveland and are proud parents and grandparents of two wonderful children and two adored grandchildren.

By contrast, David's professional life followed two distinctly different directions. The first was in business, notably as employee communication director for Marriott Corporation. His later and longer role was in academia, where he held faculty positions in the communication and business schools at Cal State Fullerton and USC, then as MBA director at the University of Arkansas. Now also retired, David and his wife Karen reside in Oceanside, California, near one of their two children and two of their four grandchildren. Like Rick, David is an avid photographer, a huge baseball fan and an ardent world traveler.

. . . .

For more on the *Sons of Suicide* project, including resources for those seeking help, a Q&A with the authors, suggested group and book club discussion questions, data on suicide trends, articles and commentaries, go to:

http://sonsofsuicidebook.com

. . . .